# More Everyday Parables

. . . Simple Stories for
Spiritual Reflection

*To Sulee*
*with love*
*James Taylor*

James Taylor

⚓

**WoodLake**

Editor: Ellen Turnbull
Cover and interior design: Chaunda Daigneault &
                           Verena Velten
Proofreader: Dianne Greenslade

WoodLake is an imprint of Wood Lake Publishing,
Inc. Wood Lake Publishing acknowledges the financial
support of the Government of Canada, through the
Book Publishing Industry Development Program
(BPIDP) for its publishing activities. Wood Lake
Publishing also acknowledges the financial support of
the Province of British Columbia through the Book
Publishing Tax Credit.

At Wood Lake Publishing, we practise what we publish,
being guided by a concern for fairness, justice, and equal
opportunity in all of our relationships with employees
and customers. Wood Lake Publishing is committed to
caring for the environment and all creation. Wood Lake
Publishing recycles, reuses, and encourages readers to do
the same. Resources are printed on 100% post-consumer
recycled paper and more environmentally friendly ground-
wood papers (newsprint), whenever possible. A percentage
of all profit is donated to charitable organizations.

**Library and Archives Canada Cataloguing in Publication**
Taylor, James, 1936-
     More everyday parables : simple stories for spiritual
reflection / James Taylor.
Includes index.
ISBN 978-1-55145-587-7

     1. Christian life–Meditations.  I. Title.
BV4832.2.T3875 2010        248        C2010-904836-9

Published by WoodLake
An imprint of Wood Lake Publishing Inc.
9590 Jim Bailey Road, Kelowna, BC, Canada, V4V 1R2
www.woodlakebooks.com
250.766.2778

Printing 10 9 8 7 6 5 4 3 2 1
Printed in Canada by
Transcontinental

**Photo Credits**

Cover: © iStock

Dreamstime.com
p. 16 © Milos Jokic
p. 30 © Cristina Bernhardsen
p. 70 © Jostein Hauge
p. 99 © Raycan

Wikimedia Commons
p. 21 Liz Lawley
p. 22 Jean-Pol GRANDMONT
p. 32 Nick Russill
p. 92 Matti Mattila
p. 129 Angela Powers

stock.xchng
p. 36 John Hughes
p. 44 Dave Dyet
p. 50 Alan Bridges
p. 54 stock.xchng
p. 58 stock.xchng
p. 62 Christopher Thiemet
p. 72 Leszek Nowak
p. 76 Herman Brinkman
p. 78 Adrian van Leen
p. 82 Michelle Vipond
p. 94 Nick Cowie
p. 104 Abdulaziz Almansour
p. 108 stock.xchng
p. 116 Jennifer Smith
p. 124 Horton Group
p. 132 Kym McLeod

p. 87 © iStockPhoto

p. 112 © ImageAfter.com

p. 38 © NASA, ESA, and
      A. Riess (STScl/JHU)

# CONTENTS

## Human Activities

## Miscellaneous Parables

# Acknowledgements and Dedication

There are so many people without whom this book would never have happened.

My list starts with Ralph Milton, who talked me into joining him in founding Wood Lake Books, way back in 1981.

It continues with all the employees of that fledgling publishing company, who kept it going through some very lean years – and even a few prosperous ones.

It includes my wife, Joan, whose regular income was about all that enabled me to keep working at publishing books through those lean years, and who tolerated my obsession with turning out a quality product even when it meant working long hours into the night.

For this particular book, I have to thank Jack McCarthy and Bud Mortenson, publisher and editor respectively of the Lake Country *Calendar* newspaper during the early 1990s. They invited me to start writing a column for their paper. As I recall it, I had gone for about a year without writing anything for publication. My mind felt it was stagnating – I had no reason for paying attention to the events and activities swirling around me. Jack and Bud got me thinking again. The columns I wrote for them form the foundation of most of the parables included in this book.

But mostly, I think of Mike Schwartzentruber. When Wood Lake Books had only existed for about three years, Mike called me. He said he had written a book about the experience of living with cystic fibrosis. Would we consider publishing it?

I said no. My own son had died of cystic fibrosis just six months before. Something in Mike's husky breathless voice sounded too much like my son's voice. I didn't think I could face the constant reminder while working with Mike.

But Mike and his friends didn't give up. I went to see Mike in his hospital bed, apparently just days from death. He was, incredibly, in the same bed, in the same room, where my son had died. I could not say no.

Mike recovered and Wood Lake published his book *From Crisis to New Creation*.

After Mike had a double lung transplant in 1990, his wife asked him, "What do you want to do, now that you've got your life back?"

"I want to edit with Jim Taylor," Mike replied.

And he did.

Mike is now president of Wood Lake Publishing.

I thought I was through writing books. I thought I was growing old. I thought it was enough work writing two newspaper columns a week – one for the *Calendar*, another for the Kelowna weekend paper. Then Mike called me about doing a second volume of *Everyday Parables*. And again, I could not say no.

So, on this 20th anniversary of the lung transplant that gave him new life, I dedicate this book to Mike Schwartzentruber. With thanks.

# INTRODUCTION

This is my second book of parables.

Why parables? Because they were Jesus' way of communicating his message. He didn't provide learned lectures. He told parables.

We, tragically, have turned his message into dogma. We expound theology. We string together this verse and that in an attempt to prove that there is a single coherent system connecting writings that happened 1000 years apart. We turn the Bible into a coded message, a jigsaw puzzle that must be put together in just the right way to make sense. Jesus would have been appalled.

## Spontaneous inventions

My first book of parables was based on Jesus' simpler parables, which are really extended figures of speech.

Teachers in those days didn't have classrooms with digital projectors and PowerPoint presentations. They tended to be itinerant, walking through the country, gathering students wherever they went. So I see Jesus walking through the fields with a small knot of disciples surrounding him.

If you look at Luke 13, you find a series of parables about everyday objects: a fig tree, a mustard seed, yeast, a narrow door... And in the middle of it, this line: "Jesus went through one town and village after another, teaching as he made his way to Jerusalem."

His students, his disciples, kept pestering him about this strange thing he called the kingdom of God. They didn't see any signs of a throne, or rich carpets, or silk cushions and gold utensils, or any of the pomp and luxury that marked worldly monarchies. The disciples wanted to know when the luxury and power was going to come their way. They didn't understand.

So Jesus looked for examples as he walked along. In the middle of a field, he saw a mustard bush. And he ad libbed a metaphor about a mustard seed. "It's like a tiny seed," he said. "But look what it can grow into!"

A little later, they passed through a village. A village woman had come out to sit on her front step while kneading dough for the family's daily bread.

"It's like the yeast in that bread dough," Jesus said. "Just a little yeast permeates the entire dough. In the same way, the kingdom that I'm talking about permeates every aspect of life."

The gospels list about 50 parables that Jesus told. Many of those are the kind I've just described – figures of speech that relate some commonplace event or activity to the new kind of life that Jesus promised.

My first book of parables, *Everyday Parables,* dealt entirely with that kind of parable. They were, essentially, extended metaphors. About potato peelers and gravel beaches; about jigsaw puzzles and shoelaces.

## The storyteller

But the rest of the parables that Jesus told were more than figures of speech. They were stories. They too were probably impromptu, made up on the spot, perhaps adapted from some local gossip gleaned from the marketplace as Jesus passed through.

These are the stories that everyone knows: stories about the good Samaritan, the prodigal son, the wedding banquet, the workers in the vineyard...

I didn't include story parables in *Everyday Parables.* So I decided, when I was asked to write a sequel, that I would concentrate on that second kind.

## Beyond our biblical prison

I have deliberately not simply paraphrased the old parables into modern language. We need to update our language, certainly, but even more we need to break our imagination free of its biblical prison. The Bible was written by a desert people who never really outgrew their nomad roots. They wrote about droughts, not deluges; about searing heat, not blizzards; about goats, not supermarkets.

As I wrote in the introduction to *Everyday Parables* (included as an appendix at the end of this book):

> The problem is not that the story of God, the message of Jesus, is out of date. The problem is that we Christians have been content to express that story in outdated images and metaphors.
>
> As a community of faith, the stories we tell imply that God is not present in our world. God was there in biblical times. God may have been there during the medieval period, and during the Reformation. God may be revealed in the German theological colleges of a century ago, or in the barrios and *favelas* of Latin America, or in the unspoiled wilderness of a national park. But God is not here in our four-wheel drive SUVs, our iPods, our GPS navigation systems.
>
> Because we simply do not talk about God when we talk about those things.

Yes, people still build houses on flood plains, and still lose coins, and still fail to plan for midnight emergencies. But if we limit ourselves to the illustrations that correspond with biblical narratives, we leave out a large part of our present-day experience.

I believe that God speaks to us through more than the Bible. The Bible may be about God, but if God is truly Creator, so is nature. So is science. And history. For that reason, I have included in these modern parables some events that would have been inconceivable to the gospel writers. Because I believe that if Jesus were telling parables today, he would do as he did back then – he would talk about things that people knew in their everyday lives.

## The meaning of the message

You may notice that very few of Jesus' story parables have explanations. The primary exception is the parable of the sower, told in three gospels (Matthew 13:3–9, Mark 4:1–9, Luke 8:4–8). All three gospels follow the parable with an explanation. Scholars now suggest – based on literary and historical clues – that the explanation didn't come from Jesus at all. It fits too nicely with what the developing church saw as its mandate, which was to build membership.

Most of Jesus' story parables have no explanation. We are left to figure out for ourselves what he intended us to understand. Some, like the parable of the workers in the vineyard who all get the same wage, no matter how many hours they worked, can be disturbing. Some, like the parable of the sheep and the goats, seem to require us to do "good works" for the poor and homeless.

But that's how story works – you can read into it whatever you want. *Little Red Riding Hood* is usually interpreted these days as innocence conquering evil; it could also provide justification for hunting and killing predators. *Jack and the Beanstalk* could be about foolish investments, or about the benefits of disobeying one's parents.

To complicate matters, we have often mislabelled Jesus' parables. The central character in what we call the parable of the prodigal son is really, I believe, the loving father. The younger son has, effectively, stabbed the father in the back. He has demanded his share of the family farm, something that would normally happen only when the father dies. The son has declared his father dead. It is a mortal insult.

But then the son returns. Family honour and social standards both demand that the father reject his wandering son. But the father still loves the son, despite the son's scandalous behaviour. So the father disgraces himself further by running to meet his son, by welcoming him back, by throwing a gigantic party for him.

That's the loving father that Jesus wanted us to know.

And then there's the elder son. Who has his knickers in a knot. He's jealous. He never did his father any dirt. He's been loyal, faithful, and obedient. And what does he get for this? The burden of tilling the fields, cleaning the stables, and herding ungrateful livestock. No wonder he's angry.

So which message does one take from this parable? Are we the reprobate younger son, coming home after squandering the family's wealth on drugs and sex, hoping for forgiveness? Are we the forgiver? Are we the grudge bearer, who expects to be rewarded for having kept our nose to the grindstone? Jesus doesn't tell us what his point is. Maybe it's all of those. Just possibly, it was none of them.

Which leaves me with a dilemma. Because when I choose the stories that I present as modern-day parables, I want to tell you what their meaning is. I want to be sure you don't miss the point.

But that's not what Jesus would have done.

So I've compromised. I tell the story, and you can, if you wish, stop there. You can see where and how your experience resonates with that story. You can see if it touches you at all.

Or you can carry on reading and see what I got out of it. So I've included some reflections of my own on each story. They might illuminate your thoughts; they might not.

If you read a different message from my parable-story, please let me know. Write to me at any of the following addresses:

Jim Taylor
c/o Wood Lake Publishing
9590 Jim Bailey Road
Kelowna, BC  V4V 1R2

e-mail
rewrite@shaw.ca
jimt@quixotic.ca

Putting your responses into words may help you clarify what will probably start as emotional reaction. It certainly worked that way for me, as I reflected on things that I have observed around me.

Jim Taylor

# How to Use This Book

## For personal reading

You can, of course, read this book just as you would any other book – starting from the beginning and reading through to the end. Or you can read it at random, flipping pages idly until some story or reference catches your eye, and then reading that page all by itself.

My experience with other books of this type suggests that you'll get the most benefit from a more disciplined reading, such as taking one story each day for exploration. Some people prefer to read in the morning, and then reflect on the story through the day, seeing if it illuminates their experiences that day. Others find it more helpful to read the page at night and reflect back over their day for insights into their experiences.

## For group use

But what if you're called upon to provide a "meditation" or "devotional message" for a group, or if your weekly study group is using this book as their text? I suggest that you don't merely read these parables out loud. Instead, try this process:

1. Choose a "parable."
2. Have someone read the Bible passage suggested at the end of that story.
3. Read the parable that opens each of these items.
4. Invite people to reflect, in a short period of silence, on how this story resonates with their own experience. Have they had similar experiences? What significance did they attach to that experience? Some people may wish to share their thoughts with the group.
5. Read my "musings" about the story. My reflection on the story may support the comments that others have made;

sometimes it may provide an alternate perspective. Remember that there is no single "right answer" – either to my parables or to Jesus' parables. What you get from a parable is what you get from it. Some people may wish to share their thoughts with the group.

6. Close by reading the suggested Bible passage again. You may find it offers some new insights now.

Jim Taylor

# Plants and Nature

*Jesus drew a lot of his teaching illustrations from the world of nature. He told parables about fig trees. He said that God loved sparrows. He described himself as a vine, and his disciples as branches. He used the tiny mustard seed as an analogy for the growth of God's kingdom – or kin-dom, as many prefer.*

*Jesus did not refer to gravity, or to the tidal waves that we call tsunami. Even if he knew about such things – some people insist that if he were divine as well as human, he must have had divine knowledge of such things – his hearers would have had no idea what he was talking about.*

*But that doesn't mean that we should ignore these phenomena. So I offer you some parables about our natural world.*

# Pears and People

The orchard at the far end of our road grows only pears. Nothing else.

That's a bit surprising. Most orchards today produce a variety of fruit. The Okanagan valley used to be almost exclusively an apple area. Apples show up on everything from shopping centre logos to municipal mottos. But apples are less important than they once were. Many apple orchards are moving into late cherries, or converting to vineyards.

But this particular orchard continues to grow pears on old, gnarled trees.

From the little that I know about fruit-growing, pears are an unforgiving tree fruit. Pears have to be picked long before they're ripe. If you wait until they're ripe to pick them, they have a "best-before date" that lasts about 15 minutes.

I had a pear tree, once. When the pears were just ripe, they were utterly delicious. The skin split easily; the flesh melted in my mouth; the sweet nectar dribbled down my chin. The day before, though, they were as hard as if carved out of marble. And even an hour later those pears would have started to rot at the core.

The owner of this old orchard still sticks to pears. He was up a tree, thinning his crop, as I walked by.

For those who don't have much acquaintance with orchards, thinning does not involve putting obese pears on a diet. It means selectively removing excess fruit – any kind of fruit – from every branch. A tree's root system can supply only so much nourishment. If a branch has too many pieces of fruit on it, the tree will divide that available energy too thinly; each branch will produce a host of undersized, and therefore underpriced, fruit. The combined weight of too much fruit can also snap a branch, thus denying the farmer a harvest from that branch not only this year, but every year to come.

Because it involves making choices, thinning can't be easily mechanized. Leaving only the most promising fruit to continue growing is a tedious job, done best by hand.

"You'd think," I suggested facetiously to the guy up the tree, "that the good Lord could have designed trees better able to care for themselves, wouldn't you?"

He laughed. "The good Lord may have other things on his mind," he replied.

There was a moment's silence. Then he added, "Sometimes I think God put these trees here as a test."

I must have muttered something that conveyed lack of comprehension.

"You know," he explained, "to see if we humans care enough to look after them properly."

I was still digesting that little bit of wisdom when he added one last comment. "Especially these old trees," he said. "I could replant new varieties that don't need as much maintenance. But I keep these trees because I love them."

## Musings

As I walked on, it occurred to me that God might be saying something very similar about us humans.

Perhaps we too could be replaced by something that would produce more of the kind of fruitful actions that God wants. After all, we pray, "Your will be done, on earth as in heaven…"

We certainly can't claim that we have never caused any trouble for God. The Bible is full of stories of how we humans miss the point, take the wrong paths, let God down. God would probably be entirely justified in bulldozing our orchard and starting over – as God apparently did, in the story of Noah.

But maybe God promised never to do that again because God loves us the way we are.

**Bible reading:** Genesis 6:5–7, 9:8–11.
God's covenant with Noah.

# GOODBYE TO EDEN

Snow had fallen softly all night.

In the pearly dawn, the new snow lay deep and silent. No one – no one at all – had left so much as a mark in it. The tiniest twigs had muffs of snow balanced delicately upon them. Every tree, every shrub, was etched in black and white. It felt as if the usual cluttered and untidy colour snapshot of daily life had somehow been exchanged for an Ansell Adams art print.

I knew that I ought to be revelling in all this breathless beauty. And at one level, I was. But at another level, I wanted to stay snuggled under the covers in my warm bed.

It's not the first time I have felt this tension between adventure and comfort. Back in my university days, I worked one summer in the mountains some 50 miles inland from Kitimat on British Columbia's north coast. I spent two months in the bush without a shave, without a shower. I loved the outdoors. I loved the simplicity of life in the woods. I found it hard to believe that I was actually getting paid for living in paradise.

One evening, my trail mate and I sat by a crackling campfire. Flames licked around a pot of water warming for tea. Behind us, our tent sat comfortably in the shelter of a huge hemlock. Our underwear was washing itself in a burbling stream running by.

We heard the roar of an engine overhead. The company helicopter – a Korean War vintage Bell, the kind made familiar by episodes of M*A*S*H – landed on a gravel bar by the camp. It had come to take me back to civilization.

I went.

After I had had a hot shower and a meal I didn't have to cook, the boss offered me an office job. I took it. The seductive appeal of hot water, a soft mattress, and a roof over my head won out over unspoiled simplicity.

## Musings

Perhaps it has always been so. I suspect that's the real message behind the ancient story of the Garden of Eden. If you set aside all the scholarly quibbles about the order of creation, the origins of evil, and the meaning of having dominion over nature, the story tells us that we can't go back.

I wonder how many times, later in life, as Adam sweated in his fields, as Eve screamed in childbirth, they dreamed of the idyllic life they had once enjoyed. But they couldn't go back.

Very few people have the courage and conviction to turn their backs on the allure of luxury. Choosing to deliberately do without is different from being forced to. Many people make do with old cars, shabby clothing, or skimpy housing because they have no choice. But very few voluntarily choose to do without labour-saving appliances like automatic washers and dryers, or to stay home instead of taking faraway holidays, to work only with hand tools, or to deny themselves the benefits of modern medical treatment.

Given a choice between an early morning snowfall and a warm bed, I know which one I would choose, every time.

---

**Bible reading:** Genesis 3:16–24.
Banished from the Garden of Eden.

# LEAVING A LEGACY

If the community I live in has a symbolic plant, it must be the tree of heaven, *Ailanthus altissima*, also known as the copal tree or varnish tree.

Although it's endemic in our small corner of the world, I rarely see it elsewhere. Apparently, it comes originally from China and was brought to Philadelphia in 1784 by an avid gardener named William Hamilton. Since then, the spread of the tree of heaven has been rivalled only by that of starlings. Around 1890, Eugene Schieffelin released 60 pairs of European starlings in New York's Central Park. He wanted to introduce into North America all the birds mentioned in the writings of Shakespeare. His attempts to import bullfinches, chaffinches, nightingales, and skylarks failed. But Schieffelin's starlings have become, by one description, "one of the most spectacular environmental disruptions ever perpetrated by an individual."

But back to the tree of heaven. Residents in urban areas like the tree because it grows fast and resists pollution. *Ailanthus altissima* formed the central metaphor of the novel *A Tree Grows in Brooklyn*.

When I first arrived here 17 years ago, I looked down from our deck and saw several magnificent specimens of the tree in the yards below us, their domed crowns covered with reddish-ochre or pale yellow blossoms. I wanted one. I planted a shoot at one end of our property.

Too late, I learned that most botanists consider *Ailanthus altissima* a weed. Not only does it scatter seeds by the thousands, it sends out sucker roots that tunnel along just under the surface. They exude an organic herbicide that inhibits competing native plants. And what roots! Cleaning up the corner of my yard, I ripped out roots 20 feet long.

Once a weed like the tree of heaven gains a foothold, it tends to take over.

## Musings

Every since biblical times, people have equated weeds with sin. Jesus told parables about weeds choking healthy plants, about sorting weeds from wheat at harvest time. Subsequent moralists have taught that sins, like weeds, must be totally rooted out, eradicated, stomped on, sprayed with weed killer – anything to eliminate them – and replaced with beneficial things.

That analogy breaks down when we remember that our beneficial plants were once weeds, too. Wheat and barley were wild grasses; cucumbers and tomatoes were wild vines. Even today, if you give a zucchini a free hand, it will take over your garden.

I used to think of weeds as unwanted plants. But that's too subjective – after all, I *wanted* this particular tree of heaven inhabiting a corner of my lot. And some weeds can be stunningly beautiful. The wild blossoms that grace alpine meadows are, technically, all weeds.

So I suggest an alternate definition. A weed is a plant that doesn't know its place.

Fortunately, that analogy fits for sin, too. There's little wrong with most sins, if they stay in their place. There's not much risk in gambling a few pennies on a card game, having an occasional drink with friends (unless you're already addicted to alcohol), or flirting mildly with an associate. The problem comes when the gambling, drinking, and/or flirting get out of control.

It's only when something starts taking over your garden – or your life – that it needs to be ripped out by the roots.

---

**Bible reading:**   Matthew 13:24–30.
                     The weeds among the wheat.

# BLESSINGS AND CURSES

Fifty kilometres away, I could see the smoke rising from the forest fire. As I drew closer, the pillar of smoke grew thicker and heavier, a grey-green gout rising into the sky, spreading at the top like an anvil, casting a pall of fear all through the valley.

I was coming home late in the evening after a week of hiking in the Rocky Mountains, near Banff. While I had been away I had heard no news reports about the forest fires raging throughout British Columbia that hot, dry summer. Now it looked as though I would soon get a first-hand introduction to them.

I turned off the highway towards my home. As I topped the ridge, I involuntarily slammed on the brakes. I thought I was looking straight into the fires of hell itself.

Across the lake, the entire hillside seemed to be ablaze. The setting sun glowed eerily through clouds of smoke. The pine forests on the shaded slope were dark, almost black – that is, the few parts that weren't on fire. Every few seconds, a tree exploded into flames, a sudden gush of red billowing up into a roiling mushroom of smoke lit from beneath.

The fire ended happily, I suppose, from a human perspective. Rain and cooler weather combined to dampen the fire's ardour. The lake separated the larger settlements from the fire and no homes were burned or human lives lost. But for a week, bits of charred bark, blackened pine needles, and grey ash settled on our deck.

For a week, we were quite afraid.

## Musings

We humans have a fascination with fire. We can sit for hours staring into a campfire, sharing stories. We barbecue over artificial embers; we gather in community to feast on seared sacrifices. We build kilns for pottery and smelters for ore. We weld and braze and solder, cauterize and sterilize, incinerate and bake.

Perhaps we remember, deep in our collective memory, that fire was the first of nature's forces to be tamed. Ancient ancestors brought a few glowing embers home, added tinder and fuel, fanned the flames into life, and suddenly humans had light and warmth.

Perhaps we also realize, at some subconscious level, that blessings and curses are closely related. Fire can keep our homes comfortable; fire can destroy our homes in seconds. We cook with fire; we can be cooked by fire. And we also know that the absence of fire can mean death, especially in frigid northern winters.

Perhaps we recognize, intuitively, that too much fire and too little fire are equally hazardous to human well-being. Only the right amount, somewhere between the two extremes, is beneficial.

The same principle applies to other factors. The right dosage of medication brings health; too much or too little brings death. Too much and too little water are equally hazardous; in one we die from drowning, with the other we die from dehydration. Too much food causes obesity; too little results in starvation.

The principle applies even to love – too little love results in neglect, too much love smothers. Like Goldilocks, we need to find a middle ground that is "just right." The dilemma has always been determining how much is "just right." How much gasoline do we really need to ignite in our cars? How much fossil fuel do we need to burn to generate electricity?

Generally, we tend to assume that if one is good, two must be better. So we seek more horsepower. More appliances. More money. More control.

Forest fires remind us that even good things, taken to an extreme, may not be good for us.

---

**Bible reading:** Revelation 18:8–10.
Babylon fallen into fire.

# FIXED FOCUS

I've been watching an old stump rot.

Before you suggest that I need greater stimulation in my life, let me explain. Since we moved here 17 years ago, I've walked a dog along the waterfront almost every day. This particular stump stands where my current dog expects to receive a treat. So I rest her leash on top of the stump while I dig a cookie out of my pocket. This gives me ample opportunity to observe the stump's progressive deterioration.

The stump's bark has been flaking away. Its hard outer layers have been cracking. At the same time, its inner core has slumped. What was once solid wood has sunk almost an inch. Someday, that core will collapse and leave only a shell standing upright. Someday, even that outer shell will disintegrate. Eventually, only a soil analyst will be able to determine that a tree once grew there.

That old stump reminds me how restricted our sense of time is. If I had not been going past there, day after day, year after year, I would see that stump as an unchanging object. Generally speaking, if I can't see something moving – during the few moments in which I pay attention – I think of it as fixed, permanent.

But over 17 years, I have seen that stump changing. It may not be alive. But it is evolving – in bits and pieces, but still evolving – towards a different state.

## Musings

The stump makes me wonder how many other things that I think of as fixed and permanent I could see changing if I paid attention.

I think of glass as solid. But my chemistry professor taught me that glass will sag if left alone for long enough. Glass is actually a very slow-moving fluid.

I think of rock as solid. But when I hike in the Rocky Mountains, I can see how layers of rock have been folded and twisted over eons. Cliffs collapse. Rivers carve mighty canyons.

I think of humans as having been around forever. But in the history of the planet, we have existed for less time than the single tick of a clock. We also assume that we will be around forever. But that too may be no longer than another tick of the clock.

On a larger time scale, it seems nothing remains unchanged. Even the universe is constantly in flux. We know that now; we didn't know it a few centuries ago.

Why, then, would we cling to a belief that God must be unchanging?

Perhaps we make a sacred/secular division – we expect the divine to differ totally from everything else that we know. Or perhaps we really believe that people 2,000 years ago, who knew far less about the universe, must have understood more about God.

I prefer to think in terms that correspond more closely to my life experience. I'm changing. My world is changing. I like to think of God as an integral part of that process, rather than being isolated from it.

---

**Bible reading:** Hebrews 6:17–20a.
An unchangeable promise.

# Of Seeds and Sowers

It looked like it was snowing outside the other day, except for the warm spring sun beaming down. There were white flakes drifting in the air, settling into the fresh growing grass, and blowing in the wind.

It was, of course, the cottonwood trees dispersing more fluffy seeds than the dollars involved in the 2009 bailouts.

Before the cottonwoods, the Chinese elms scattered their seeds wildly, profligately. And after the cottonwoods, the maples will do the same. As will dandelions, milkweed, and who knows what other plants.

It all seems colossally inefficient. You'd think that if God were smart enough to design every detail of the universe, as the proponents of intelligent design argue, God would be smart enough to figure out a less wasteful system. I mean, look what happens.

Some of the seeds fall on paved roads, where they cannot possibly establish roots. The cars drive over and crush the seeds; the rain washes them into the sewers; the sun bakes them dry.

Other seeds fall on rocky ground, like the gravel beaches along our lake. There's water there, but no soil. The seeds germinate, but the sprouts quickly wither in the sun, and wash away when storm waves sluice along the shore.

Still other seeds fall among thorns and weeds. The other plants have a head start. They grab more of the rain and block the sunshine; they choke out the struggling seedlings.

Only a small percentage of the seeds fall on good soil. Each germinating seed sends down tiny roots that gather nutrients. The small plant gains strength and establishes itself as a thriving young tree. And in time, that tree too will flower and form seeds, multiplying itself not just thirty or sixty or a hundred times, but millions of times.

Then it will scatter those seeds just as indiscriminately, as extravagantly, as its parent tree did – on roads and rocks, among weeds and thorns. Most seeds will fail to thrive. But again, a few seeds will fall on fertile soil, and start the process once more.

## Musings

What's that you say? You think you've heard this story before?

You have. It's called the *Parable of the Sower,* and it's told in all three of the synoptic Gospels.

But I think that whoever wrote the parable and added an explanation might have missed the original point. In the Gospels, Jesus' explanation comes across as self-congratulation by the disciples and other followers. They saw themselves as the "good soil," so that any teachings Jesus planted in them would produce a rich harvest.

That's a natural reaction. If seeds could think – a point on which I won't attempt to expand – any seed that settles on fertile topsoil would probably congratulate itself on being the chosen vehicle for passing life along.

But at its heart, I think, the parable is about how God works. God does not dispense gifts one by one to those who will generate the best returns. Rather, God works like those cottonwood trees. God scatters possibilities wildly, extravagantly, without regard for race or creed, status or gender. And then waits to see where those seeds will take root.

---

**Bible reading:** Mark 4:1–9.
The Parable of the Sower.

# Northern Lights

One night, I wandered outside just before bedtime. At first I thought I saw a thin veil of cloud stretched between me and the distant icy stars. Then I realized that if it were cloud, it had a million multicoloured flashlights flickering across it.

It wasn't cloud at all. It was the northern lights, the *aurora borealis*.

Usually we see the northern lights shimmering low along the horizon. But this particular night, the most spectacular display was high overhead. At times, it glowed quietly. Other times, it erupted like a volcano, firing flares right across the dome of the heavens.

As I stared up into the sky, getting a serious crick in my neck, I tried to find the right words to describe the spectacle. Scientific explanations about solar flares and charged ions and magnetic fields simply don't cut it when you're gazing in awe at a mystery. In my imagination, I saw it as surf surging up a heavenly beach and then retreating. Or like sheer curtains, shifting in a breeze. Like sunlight, reflecting off the ripples of a lake. Like flames leaping from a campfire. Like autumn leaves, drifting and eddying.

None of my word pictures seemed sufficient.

Years ago, a group of fathers and sons at Scout camp lay on our backs in a field watching a similar display of the *aurora borealis* going on overhead. The father next to me voiced the best metaphor I've yet heard. "Heaven," he said reverently, "is having an orgasm."

### Musings

Anytime we humans see something that transcends our comprehension, we're forced into figures of speech – into metaphors and similes and analogies. When we don't have the words to describe the phenomenon, we resort to the formula, "It was like…"

And we all understand that this merely reflects our attempt to define the indefinable. No one assumes that the northern lights really *are* surf, leaves, or curtains. Or orgasms, for that matter.

We do the same thing when we use language about the divine, in any religion. We have to resort to figurative language. So a god may be as invisible as the wind. Fierce like an eagle. As tender as a mother.

In the Bible, Ezekiel saw his God as constant change, like the whirling wheels of a chariot. Moses encountered God as a burning bush. Jesus' disciples experienced God's spirit as something like wind and fire.

All of these are, necessarily, approximations – attempts to explain the inexplicable, to illuminate what remains essentially a mystery. They are like groping in the dark for a light switch. Unfortunately, too many people take these gropings as literal descriptions. Pentecost equals tongues of fire. Moses could have toasted marshmallows at his bush. And Erich von Däniken turned Ezekiel's chariot into a book about extraterrestrial visitors.

Why, I wonder, does our Western society have so much difficulty dealing with figurative language? We seem to want everything as cut and dried as pressed flowers laminated in plastic. We want perceptions to add up as precisely as a column of figures.

Some things don't.

Some things never will.

---

**Bible reading:** Acts 2:1–4.
The coming of the Holy Spirit.

# BURIED SCARS

I was splitting wood for the fireplace earlier this month.

There's something very satisfying about splitting – the grip of my hands on the polished axe handle, the strain of muscles in my arms and shoulders, the power of the axe head whirling down. When a log splits cleanly, the two halves spring apart like greyhounds leaping from the starting gate; the wood rings like a xylophone.

One log looked promising. On the outside, I could see no sign of knots.

My first swing made about as much impression on the log as it would have on reinforced concrete.

I swung again. The axe head bit deeply into the grain. And stuck there. I had to pry it out.

I swung again. Eventually, I wore the log out. In sheer weariness, it split. And deep inside, I found the problem. At some time early in that tree's life, it had been wounded. There had been a limb broken or pruned off. The tree had grown around the amputated stump until the outside bark looked unblemished.

But deep inside, the grain still contorted around the invisible scar.

## Musings

Communities can be like that, too.

A while ago, a controversy split our local community. At a community meeting, one speaker burst out passionately, "I used to love coming home. As soon as I came over the ridge, it felt like a haven of peace. I don't feel that anymore. This kind of thing just tears me up..."

The issue has now passed into history. The divisions seem to have healed over. On the surface, at

least, things have returned to normal. But if some-time in the future someone who doesn't know about that former scar tampers with the status quo, they will re-open an old wound and wonder why they got such a hostile reaction.

People have different ways of dealing with conflict.

Some want to drag everything out into the open. To get it resolved once and for all. They usually assume that – with sufficient confrontation or persuasion – the other side will have to admit they were wrong. This process forces someone to lose. And a different scar forms.

Others say we should forget it. Sweep it under the carpet. Let wounds gloss over. But the knot still hides deep within the wood.

Personally, I hate conflict. I go out of my way to avoid it. But when I get backed into a corner, I tend to come out fighting, hoping to do as much damage to my opponent as possible before I go down.

The obvious answer is not to get into conflict in the first place. That would require fully hearing the other side. It would mean listening to other view-points. It would mean treating other people's views with respect. Sometimes it might mean changing one's mind and not doing what one had intended to do, so as to honour the collective consensus.

If it's done properly, we don't have to grow a hard knot deep inside the community.

---

**Bible reading:** Matthew 5:21–24.
Make peace with your brother or sister.

# THE LAW OF GRAVITY

When I take the dog out for her morning walk, I usually lead her down a steep little path at the end of our road. The path used to be just mud. A few years ago, the local municipality decided to improve it. They smoothed out the bumps, enhanced the drainage, and brought in several truckloads of gravel that they spread evenly over the full length of the trail.

But the top end of the trail has no gravel left on it anymore. Some of it got moved by erosion, as rainwater rushed down the slopes. Most of it got moved by the simple force of gravity. When I walk the path, every time I put my heel down it crunches a small mound of gravel ahead of it. Thousands of footfalls have moved the overlay of gravel steadily downhill.

Gravity does more than just make apples drop on Isaac Newton's head. It causes water to flow downhill, carving ravines and canyons. It causes cliffs to crumble. It holds a thin skin of atmosphere around the earth and keeps the earth and other planets in stable orbit around the sun.

The sun is not only the anchor point for our solar system. It is the source of life. Everything on this earth – plants, animals, insects, fish, and yes, humans too – depends on the sun for life. Without the sun, there would be no plants and no photosynthesis. Without the sun, water would not evaporate, form clouds, fall as rain, run as rivers, or be available to irrigate our fields. Without the sun, earth would be a sterile rock hurtling through frozen space. Even the fossil fuels that our industrial civilization depends on are simply forms of solar energy that fell on the earth millions of years ago.

Yet the sun itself was formed by gravity. Gravity compressed the solar gases until they ignited the fusion furnace that still gives us light and heat.

Not even light escapes the clutches of an astronomical black hole. But gravity does.

Gravity is omnipresent.

## Musings

Around the time of Moses, the ancient Egyptians worshipped a single god – the sun god Ra. Their Pharaoh had recognized that all the other gods (of wind, fertility, river, storm, etc.) depended on a single source of heat and light: the sun.

The ancient Egyptians didn't – and probably couldn't – recognize that the sun itself was formed by the invisible force of gravity.

Physicists say that compared to the "strong force" that holds atomic nuclei together, the force of gravity is considered very weak. Yet gravity surrounds us, envelops us, so completely, so universally, that most of us are completely unaware of its presence.

I find myself thinking that might also be a pretty good description of God.

---

**Bible reading:** Acts 17:24–28.
The one in whom we live and move and have our being.

# FOOLHARDY ACTIONS

After the tsunami in the Indian Ocean at Christmas 2004, I was reminded of my own experience with a tsunami. I was working at a radio station in Prince Rupert, on the northern British Columbia coast. Not many years before, a huge earthquake in Alaska had sent a tidal wave surging down the coast, causing major damage in communities like Port Alberni.

The call came to the radio station from the tsunami warning network. Alaska had had another tremor. A tsunami could be on its way. We broadcast an alert that advised people to stay away from the shore during the afternoon.

My boss handed me a portable tape recorder ("portable," in those days, meant anything under 20 pounds) and told me, "Go get a story."

"Why me?" I demanded. "I'm office staff, not a news reporter."

"Because everyone else is on shift in the studios, and I'm not going to call someone in on overtime," he replied.

I lugged the equipment down to a floating dock near the harbour entrance. A few minutes before the tsunami was scheduled to arrive, I started dictating my observations into the tape recorder.

Prince Rupert has huge tides. They can vary 27 feet between high and low water. The ocean rushes in and out of the harbour so fast that some boats cannot make headway against it. They wait until the tide turns to enter or leave.

I remember watching the green seaweed attached to the pilings that held the dock in place. As the tide rushed out of the harbour, the seaweed tendrils streamed out towards the open ocean. Then the tide switched and flowed back into the harbour for about ten minutes. Then it rushed back out towards the ocean again.

That's all the tsunami amounted to. No crashing surf, no wall of water surging up the channel, no vast outwash sucking bodies out to sea. Yet it was strong enough to reverse that massive tidal flow for about ten minutes.

As I look back, I wonder what kind of idiot would go and sit where the effect of the tsunami would have been greatest, if it had happened.

## Musings

What kind of fool would believe he was immune to nature's power? All of us, I suspect.

Somehow, we all believe that we are immortal, although we might not all apply that title to our belief. Particularly when we're young, we're convinced we can safely survive blizzards, car accidents, and barroom brawls. So I doubt that many of us read about the disaster in the Indian Ocean and thought, "I would be dead now." Rather, each of us took for granted that while thousands of others might die, we would survive to tell the tale.

We hear about an airline crash, and expect that we would survive. We hear about an earthquake in Haiti, Chile, or Pakistan, and imagine ourselves working to dig others out of the debris. We rarely if ever imagine ourselves perishing in the rubble.

In the 1600s, English poet Edward Young caught that notion: "All men think all men mortal, but themselves." Or as a psychologist put it more abstractly, "We cannot imagine our own non-existence."

Delusions of immortality may well lie beneath our most foolhardy acts, with war topping the list. Conversely, awareness of our own mortality may be the beginning of wisdom.

**Bible reading:** Psalm 103:15–18.
Mortality.

# ANIMALS AND BIRDS

*Biologists divide living things into two great groups – plants and animals. In that classification, mosquitoes are animals. So are fish, snakes, and intestinal parasites.*

*Most of us don't have much feeling of kinship with those creatures. We feel closer to birds and mammals – basically, to the creatures we tend to keep as pets.*

*Back in biblical times, people didn't keep many pets. If I can trust a concordance published by Oxford University Press, which should be fairly reliable, cats are never mentioned in the Bible. Dogs are mentioned only in a derogatory sense as untrustworthy scavengers and carrion-eaters, much as we might speak of hyenas or buzzards.*

*As a result, there are no biblical parables about household pets. The closest thing to any teaching based on domesticated animals is the Canaanite woman's response to Jesus: "Even the dogs under the table get to eat the children's crumbs." (Mark 7:28)*

*Jesus does indicate that God loves sparrows. But it's in the sense that God loves* even *sparrows, the least of the animals acceptable for ritual sacrifice at the Jerusalem temple. "Are not five sparrows sold for two pennies?" Jesus asks. "Yet not one of them is forgotten in God's sight." (Luke 12:6)*

*But if people back then didn't have pets, people today certainly do. Indeed, we often treat our pets better than society treats some of its human members. A visitor from the Caribbean island of Tobago commented, "If there is such a thing as reincarnation, I want to come back as a Canadian dog."*

*To leave out parables about our pets – feathered or furry – would be to exclude a large portion of our lives from religious insight.*

# Soaring Fearlessly

We expected to spend a lazy week on a relatively undeveloped Caribbean island. We exceeded our expectations.

Indeed, we did so little that I spent a fair portion of each day watching a seabird circle over the ocean until she saw fish under the surface. Then she folded her wings and plummeted into the water like a feathered projectile. Seconds later, she popped up again – sometimes to resume her aerial circles, sometimes to pause long enough to swallow her catch before becoming airborne again.

And I found myself envying her. Not for spending all day, every day, circling endlessly over the same patch of sea, hoping to consume half her weight in fish each day. Rather, I envied her absence of fear. She would, naturally, head for safety if a hawk or eagle neared. But she clearly had no fear of flying. She wheeled and swooped with complete confidence in her own abilities, adjusting her flight with tiny twitches of wingtip feathers.

I would love to fly. I could take flying lessons. But at my age, I don't trust my reflexes, and even if I passed I would live with a constant fear of getting into a situation where my mistake could cost lives. When you make a mistake in an airplane, you can't get out and walk home.

The seabird has no such fear. She cannot exceed her capabilities. Even if she makes a mistake in a tight turn, she will only fall a few feet in a flurry of feathers before she can regain her composure, spread her wings, and soar again. Natural air resistance prevents her falling faster than she can recover.

So she soars fearlessly.

## Musings

By contrast, the primary motivation of humans may well be fear. We work like slaves for an employer we loathe because we fear unemployment. Advertising uses fear to sell us cosmetics, pills, diets, dating services, tutoring programs, security systems, and much more.

Advertising preaches a doctrine of conditional love. If you buy this car, if you use this cosmetic, if you follow this leader, then you will be admired, beautiful, and respected. We may proclaim God's unconditional love, but we don't manifest that conviction in our rush to purchase things that we believe will make us more acceptable.

Politics in particular foments fear, encouraging suspicion of parties and policies, of leaders we still don't know or know too well, of other countries and nationalities. For nine years now, the entire American nation has been manipulated by fear of terrorists who may or may not exist. Communism may be a spent force, even in China, but anti-communism lives on in phobias about a nebulous evil called "socialism."

Fear paralyzes. We fear saying the wrong thing, wearing the wrong clothes, holding the wrong ideas. We fear relationships that go sour; we may even fear relationships that grow too close. We become what British author Mark Gibbs once called "God's frozen people."

If we could banish some of our fears perhaps we too could soar effortlessly.

---

**Bible reading:** Isaiah 40:28–31.
Rise on wings like eagles.

# THE GENTLE GIANT

Once, when I was about eight, I saw a horse kick a man. I don't know if the horse had a bad temper, or if the man had mistreated his mount. But as the man passed behind the horse on a mountain trail, the horse coiled up both hind legs and struck out. Its hooves caught the man squarely in the chest and catapulted him right off the trail and down the slope below.

He must have had several broken ribs. Perhaps more. I didn't stay to watch. I ran from the scene as fast as my terrified eight-year-old legs could carry me.

Later in life, I took a group of Scouts to visit the police stables at Sunnybrook Park in Toronto. I mentioned that incident to the sergeant guiding us around, as an explanation for my fears of horses.

"They're just so powerful," I said.

He looked surprised. "They are," he agreed, as the horse behind him snuffled his ear affectionately. "Fortunately, they don't know it."

I'm getting over my fear with help from Wotan (pronounced votan), who lives down the road from us. The name Wotan is a variant spelling for Wodin, or Odin, the Norse god often depicted riding a huge eight-legged horse into battle.

Wotan is a horse. At 20 years old, he stands over 18 hands tall. That puts him in some special company. The *Guinness Book of World Records* lists the world's tallest horse at just over 20 hands (a hand measures four inches). But that horse died a year ago. The current claimant for the title is an Ontario Clydesdale named Poe, at 20.2 hands tall. Record-setter or not, Wotan is a very big horse. I stand five feet eight inches tall and I have to look up to Wotan's shoulders.

Despite his size, Wotan is amazingly gentle. He canters up to the fence when I come by and offers his head and neck for a quick rub. He could, if he wished, effortlessly kick the slats out of the fence, but he doesn't. He reminds me that it is possible to have power without needing to use it; that it is possible to have strength and still be gentle.

## Musings

Most of our images of power and strength come from two sources: the monarchy and the military.

So we think, perhaps, of Henry VIII executing a succession of wives for failing to produce a male heir to the throne, even though we now know, through studies of genetics, that the fault was his, not that of his wives. Or we think of Emperor Nero burning tarred Christians as torches for his garden parties. Lewis Carroll satirized this kind of power in *Alice in Wonderland.* The Queen of Hearts commanded, "Off with his head!" at the slightest provocation.

Or else we think of military might – of tanks and bombs and massed legions crushing opposition the way a bulldozer crushes a buttercup. That kind of power still fascinates many people. At any air show, the biggest lineups are to peer inside a jet fighter at the awesome technology.

Such images lead us to think that power must be used to be useful. What's the point of having a 400-horse-power car if you never use all that power? What value is an army if it grows fat and lazy in its barracks?

Jesus had power. The gospels attest that he had the power to heal illnesses, restore injuries, know what was happening a day's walk distant, and raise the dead. We take for granted that he also had the power to punish wrongdoers, escape from his captors, and come down from the cross.

But he didn't do those things.

Whatever power he had, he chose not to use it. Or perhaps, not to abuse it.

Like Wotan, Jesus reminds me that power is not an end in itself. It is possible to have power without using it. It is possible to have strength and still be gentle.

---

**Bible reading:** Luke 9:51–56.
Refuses to call down fire on an unfriendly village.

# ATTITUDE OF GRATITUDE

They say you can't teach an old dog new tricks. Whoever "they" are, they're wrong.

Earlier this year, we got a new dog. New to us, anyway. A year before, our first Irish setter, Brick, died. We mourned him too deeply to replace him immediately.

Then our friend Ann Affleck called us. "Do you know anyone who might like to adopt an Irish setter?" she asked.

Silly question. Three hours later, we were headed home with Phoebe in the back seat of our car.

In spite of love at first sight, we had some qualms about taking Phoebe. She was ten years old. That meant she probably didn't have too long to live. We hesitated about the prospect of watching another dog go through decline and infirmity. We weren't as worried about the dog's suffering, I have to confess, as about our own emotions.

Then we thought, if we could have had Brick for another year or two, would we have hesitated? Emphatically no! So we adopted Phoebe.

And she has been a joy. An absolute joy. She's gentle, trusting, quiet, patient, placid, and loyal. And she's beautiful. The way she dances down the road during her morning walk would make Ginger Rogers look awkward.

And an old dog can learn new tricks. In a few short weeks, she learned our set of commands – or most of them, anyway. Some, I suspect, she deliberately ignored, because they made no sense to her. She learned to get along with two irritable cats. She learned to balance herself in my jiggly little sports car, with her nose stuck out over the top of the windshield, soaking up the scent-sory extravaganza wafting by.

Even if these few months were all the time we had with her, she would still have been worth it.

## Musings

Phoebe even managed to teach some new tricks to this old dog about the meaning of thanksgiving. I have learned that it's not about being thankful for benefits received in the past – a kind of accounting that balances the good against the bad, and concludes that on the whole, the good outweighs the bad, and therefore I can afford some gratitude. Nor is it about hope for the future – a sort of thank you in advance for favours expected, in this world or the next.

Thanksgiving is about right now. It's about celebrating this moment, no matter what went before or what will come after. This moment, and then the next moment, and the next, so that all of life becomes an outpouring of gratitude.

I won't pretend that I attain that exalted state very often. I still get upset by bumbling incompetence. I grieve losses and rage at unfairness. Sometimes I despair for the future of this lovely blue-green planet.

But Phoebe manages that attitude of thanksgiving most of the time. And when I walk her on a bright autumn afternoon, and the sunshine ripples on her red coat and her tongue hangs happily out the side of her mouth, I do too. Life is good. Thanks be to God!

---

**Bible reading:** Philippians 4:4–7.
Rejoice in the Lord.

# WATCH FOR THE MAGPIES

A pair of magpies has decided to harass our cats.

Anytime either cat goes out, the magpies land nearby and squawk constantly at her. And magpies can make an amazing range of squawks. Comedian Lorne Elliott speaks of hearing what he thought was an entire menagerie of birds on the far side of a hedge. When he stuck his head through for a look, he found a single magpie.

These two magpies hop around just out of reach of the cats' claws. Somehow, the magpies know exactly how far those claws can strike – which is not very far. One of the cats is sixteen years old, and moves ponderously. The other is younger and quicker, but partly blind.

The magpies are so predictable that I can use them to find the cats. The other day little Lucky, our partly blind cat, stayed out longer than we thought she should. I went into the yard and looked for her. She's never easy to find – her dappled grey fur blends subtly into the shadows. But this time, all I had to do was listen.

The two magpies were strutting around on the lawn by the cedar hedge, squawking. Simply by their presence, they told me where I would find little Lucky. Sure enough, she lay crouched under a cedar bush, squinting nervously out below the branches at her tormentors.

## Musings

Evil, these days, has a remarkable capacity to disguise itself as good. The old days when everyone knew the difference between good and evil are long gone.

Actually, in older times, people were told which was which. We, the people, deferred to the superior knowledge of our priests, our professors, our political leaders. But with the suspicion of all authority and all institutions that emerged in the 1970s, we're no longer willing to let someone else make those value judgements for us. So we find ourselves adrift on an ocean of moral possibilities, trying to distinguish flotsam from jetsam. And they often look uncommonly alike.

Of course, everyone promotes their pet cause as good. After all, who'd promote it as evil? So how can you know the difference?

To determine whether a project, a business, a cause, is honourable or questionable, look at the kind of people it attracts. What kind of get-rich-quick-without-commitment people flock to an investment scheme? What kind of friends hang out with that door-to-door roofing sales rep? Good and evil reveal their nature by the kind of people they attract, the way a magnet attracts iron filings.

---

**Bible reading:** Luke 16:10–13.
Honesty in small things.

# STRONG ROOTS, NEW SHOOTS

A few winters ago, two migratory beavers took up temporary residence under a dock along the lakeshore.

I had no idea how much damage beavers could do. For a hundred metres on either side of their home, they felled trees. Small trees. Big trees. Some as big as, well, I'd have trouble wrapping my belt around them. They nipped off the tender top branches for their winter larder, and left the main trunks littering the beach. The foreshore looked like a clear-cut loggers' convention had passed by.

Then, come spring, the beavers moved on, to who knows where.

Some community-minded residents organized a work party to clean up the devastation. They sawed up and removed the tree trunks. They cut off the ragged stumps at ground level. The beach looked cleaner, but remarkably barren. The path along the shore that used to wander amiably among leafy trees now felt exposed.

But during the summer, a small miracle occurred. The cut-off stumps sprouted new shoots. Branches shot upwards, propelled by healthy root systems. By the end of summer, the pleasant little path meandered once more through a green and pleasant land.

## Musings

Before Christmas each year, most church congregations hear the passage from the Hebrew prophet Isaiah 11: "A shoot shall come forth from the stump of Jesse, and a branch shall grow from his roots…"

The words are usually interpreted as anticipating the birth of Jesus some 800 years later. In support of that assumption, Matthew and Luke take pains to trace Jesus' ancestry back to King David.

I prefer a broader application. Maybe Isaiah did intend to describe the long-awaited Messiah. Maybe he didn't. We have no way of knowing, 28 centuries later. But he certainly gave us a universal truth: If the roots are strong, new growth can come even out of disaster.

I see little in the Bible that suggests Jesus came into this world to start a new religion. Rather, I suspect he saw a religious landscape as barren and dead as the waterfront after the beavers had gnawed their way along it. But he believed there were roots that were still sound, still strong, and still viable. So he began a passionate attempt to revitalize his own religion, Judaism. The new faith, which we now call Christianity, came when his followers found themselves rejected as heretics and troublemakers.

Christianity is going through some difficult times these days. The mainline churches shrink; the evangelical churches come under fire for rigidity and fundamentalism.

During Advent, Christians should not passively expect someone to save them, like Cinderella waiting for a fairy godmother to rescue her from mopping floors. Instead, we should be asking ourselves the question Jesus must have asked, the question Isaiah must have asked: "Are our roots strong?"

If they are, new life will come to our churches.

**Bible reading:** Isaiah 11:1–5.
New shoots from strong roots.

# CONTRADICTORY IMPULSES

All through one winter's cold snap, we kept our bird feeder well stocked. Scrappy little finches, perky chickadees, juncos in their black monk hoods, aggressive flickers, mindless quail – all congregated to plunder our manna from heaven.

Joan and I found ourselves paying particular attention to a one-legged Steller's jay. We nicknamed him Gimpy – as a term of respect, I hasten to add. When we first saw him, his right leg hung uselessly. It trailed below him in flight and drooped limply when he perched on the feeder. He eventually lost that leg completely.

I used to think that a bird with a damaged leg was doomed. But apparently not. Gimpy got along quite well on one leg. He learned to balance his weight over that off-centre claw. He could cling erect to a swaying twig. He foraged vigorously at our feeder.

We developed a special relationship with Gimpy. Not that he (or she) knew it. But whenever Gimpy landed on our feeder, we called each other to the window to watch. We admired the brilliant blue of his plumage. We celebrated his continuing survival.

We missed him when he didn't show up the following winter.

## Musings

We humans are a mixed bag of motivations.

There seems to be something in the human psyche that wants to root for the underdog. We want Frodo the Hobbit to succeed against all odds; we identify with young Harry Potter battling the evil powers of Voldemort; we cheer for Robin Hood and Peter Rabbit. In the Christmas story, we invest our sympathy in the helpless infant in the manger, not in the legal authority of King Herod.

But at the same time, we tend to rally behind upperdogs. At political party conventions, delegates start deserting losers right after the first ballot. They want to hitch their wagon to the candidate they hope will become a star. Sports teams gain fan support as soon as they look like contenders.

It seems to be an irreconcilable paradox of human nature. But perhaps paradoxes, like the recurring anomalies that led to chaos theory, are evidence of a deeper truth.

Perhaps everything consists of polarities. The truth lies somewhere on the continuum between two extremes, but it's only those extremes that make the continuum evident to us.

So we take life for granted, until confronted by the extremes of birth or death. We assume universal ethical norms, until we're shocked by the ruthlessness of a Marc Lepine or awed by the selflessness of a Mother Teresa. We never think about the water we drink, until we suffer dehydration on a hot day or devastation by a flood.

I doubt if Gimpy indulged in introspective reflection. But I'm sure the value of having two legs never crossed his little brain until he had to get along without one.

It's not that one end of the continuum is right and therefore the other must be wrong. It's that extremes themselves are wrong – extremes of poverty or wealth; of power or powerlessness; of popularity or loneliness. Even moderation, taken to an extreme, becomes immoderate.

Like Gimpy balancing on one leg, our challenge is to find a balance.

---

**Bible reading:** Mark 3:1–5.
The man with a withered hand.

# ACTING IN UNISON

A flock of Bohemian waxwings descends on our mountain ash tree every spring. But I'm not sure that flock is the right word. Flock sounds so pastoral, so placid, so sheep-like. These birds are more like a school of sharks feeding, or tow trucks converging on a highway accident.

One minute, the tree is loaded with bright red berries. The next, it stands bare naked and shivering in the chilly wind. One year, the waxwings left two – count 'em, two! – berries on the whole tree.

And then, just as suddenly as they arrive, the waxwings lift off en masse. They circle in the sky a couple of times. And they are gone.

To me, the strange thing is that they don't seem to have a leader. Granted, one Bohemian waxwing looks pretty much like another from a distance. And I didn't have much chance to get into conversation with any of them. But it didn't look as if one bird landed on the tree and then called to the others, "Hey, come on, you guys! This stuff is good!" They all arrived at once; they all left at once. It was as if a single mind motivated them.

When they left, they swirled around in the sky. The flock formed and re-formed, like the constantly changing patterns in a kaleidoscope. First one bird was in front, then another. But they wheeled and turned together as if they weren't thirty, forty, or fifty separate birds at all, but one bird, governed by a single collective mind.

### Musings

One of my favourite biblical passages comes in Paul's letter to the Christian church at Philippi. "Let the same mind be in you," he wrote, "that was in Jesus Christ."

Put in more colloquial terms, he was saying, "If Jesus is the head of the church, then you who follow him should be so much like him that you even think like him."

Paul might be a little dismayed if he could see today's Christian churches and their members squabbling with each other. Some battles involve actions that matter in people's lives today. Others, unfortunately, are simply rehashes of abstract points of theology from past centuries that make no difference at all to anyone standing in line at a grocery store or struggling with an uncooperative computer software program.

I don't suggest that all members of a faith group should become little robots, mindlessly obeying instructions from their master's voice (like the RCA terrier on the label of old vinyl records). Bland uniformity can be as boring as an endless diet of tapioca pudding.

But think of the impact that a group would have on society if all its members could act with a single mind. If an entire community shared ideals, values, and a vision that enabled them to act in unison like that flock of waxwings, they could change the world.

**Bible reading:** Philippians 2:5–10.
Having the mind of Christ.

# GOD'S DOORKNOBS

Years ago, we had a very large and very stupid black-and-white cat named – inevitably – Sylvester.

One night Joan was home alone when she heard the back door rattle. She wondered if somebody might be trying to deliver something. But the doorbell hadn't rung. The doorknob just rattled by itself.

With images from Alfred Hitchcock's horror movies racing through her mind, Joan peeked out, half expecting to see someone from *Psycho* standing there. There was no one. No one at all.

But as she stood there, the doorknob rattled again.

Finally, she gathered enough courage to stick her face right up to the window in the door. And there, standing on his hind feet and swatting at the doorknob with a front paw, was Sylvester.

Despite his limited intelligence, somehow Sylvester understood that the doorknob had something to do with opening the door. Swatting the doorknob became a kind of ritual he performed when he wanted to come inside. And lo and behold, sometimes the door would open for him to enter.

## Musings

I suspect that Sylvester's intelligence might compare to ours in roughly the same proportion as our intelligence compares to God's. Even if I had taken the doorknob mechanism apart and carefully explained exactly how all the different parts mesh to release the catch and open the door, Sylvester could never have understood.

In the same way, even if God could slow down the universe and show us how all those stars and planets, atoms and molecules, plants, animals, and people mesh together in a coherent pattern of life, death, and new life, we could never grasp it. Like Job, awestruck before God, we would have to admit that these are "things I do not understand, things too wonderful for me to know."

Yet Sylvester found that sometimes the door did open. Whether it was opened by someone inside, or by his own jiggling of the doorknob, sometimes it opened.

In much the same way, we humans have discovered that there are special times when doors seem to open into God's presence. We sense that presence powerfully when we welcome new members into our household, in the birth of a child, or by marriage. We feel that God is somehow among us when we gather in harmony around the table. We recognize God's comforting embrace in the agony of grief.

Not every time. But often enough to know that it's possible.

And because we long for those moments, we create rituals to encourage them to happen again. So we come together to celebrate baptism, communion, and marriage. We grieve together. In a sense, we rattle God's doorknobs.

And lo and behold, sometimes the door opens.

---

**Bible reading:** Luke 22:14–20.
The Last Supper.

# On Eagle's Wings

I often see bald eagles along the lake. Sometimes they perch in the topmost branches of nearby pine trees and survey their domain with an eagle eye. (Sorry, I couldn't resist the cliché.) Sometimes they ride the rising air currents high above the shores, wingtips barely twitching to control their flight.

They're magnificent.

One morning, as I strolled along the shore of the lake, I watched a couple of ducks paddling aimlessly just offshore. They ignored me; they long ago learned that humans are not a threat.

Suddenly something whooshed past my head, much the way deadlines do. A bald eagle, a mature male, had swooped down from his vantage point on the hillside behind me on the hunt for breakfast.

With his snow white head, white tail, talons poised to strike, and a wing span that exceeded the length of my outstretched arms, he took my breath away. Indeed, had he passed any closer, he could probably have taken some of my scalp away too. I felt the downdraft from his wings ruffle my hair.

The ducks saw him just in time.

If they had tried to fly, they would have been dead ducks. (Clichés must be habit forming.) Fortunately for them, in a frantic flurry of foam they dove under the surface where the eagle could not reach them.

The eagle pulled up. His momentum carried him high into the air, where he circled for a moment waiting to see if the ducks would surface. Then he flapped away down the lake, disappointed, seeking easier prey.

## Musings

Eagles soar. Ducks waddle.

Eagles have inspired great deeds. Ducks have inspired – well, in truth, I can't think of anything ducks have inspired. Except, perhaps, laughter.

But in that setting, I realized that my sympathies lay with the ducks.

The experience leads me to guess that most of us will tend to sympathize either with the eagle or with the ducks. And that choice reveals a lot about our character.

The eagle was the symbol of imperial Rome. For good reason. Like the eagle, Roman legions struck suddenly, without warning. And they struck ruthlessly. They neither showed mercy nor expected it.

In the Palestine of Jesus' time, their opposition were the Zealots. Today, they'd probably be called terrorists. Their goal was to harass the Roman army of occupation and to inflict as much damage as possible, regardless of their own risk. By genetics, they were Jews; by attitude, they were circumcised Romans.

And into that seething cauldron of hatred came a man who identified with the ducks.

The biblical gospels may or may not be totally factual (we have only their own word for the accuracy of the stories they tell) but they are the only written record we have of this man Jesus. And I can't think of one instance in those stories where he sided with the oppressor against the victim, with the predator against the prey.

To a culture based on hate, he said, "Love."

To a culture based on vengeance, he said, "Forgive."

To a culture based on greed, he said, "Share."

No wonder the powers-that-be wanted to get rid of him.

His followers are a mixed bag. At their best, they still take the side of the victim. They lobby for the poor, the sick, the suffering. They welcome the homeless, the transients. They go into politics motivated to change unfair situations and unjust laws. They tilt at windmills, and reach for stars.

But many others still yearn to emulate the imperial eagle.

---

**Bible reading:** Luke 12:6–7.

God values even sparrows.

# The Useless Emotion

In 2002, we got a new cat in our house. We didn't really want another cat, but I felt some responsibility for this one. She was blind, you see. Because I had run over her with the car.

It happened earlier that summer. I was driving past an orchard when suddenly a little grey cat dashed out from behind the trees and raced across the road in front of me with that peculiar grace of a feline in full flight.

I slammed on the brakes. I swerved. The front wheels missed her. I was beginning to breathe a prayer of relief when I heard a thump under the rear suspension. I looked back. The cat looked like a small flattened blob of fur. She struggled to raise herself off the asphalt. Bright red bubbles of blood blew out of her nose.

I got out of the car and went back and picked her up gently in my arms, hoping to carry her to her home. I went first to the house she had been dashing towards. "Not mine," said the man brusquely, and closed the door.

The folks on the other side of the road, the direction the cat had come from, were having a party. She wasn't their cat either, but they wiped the blood off her face. They called the vet's office on the chance he might be working late. He was.

"Bring her in," Dr. Eliot Kaplan told me.

I phoned the veterinary office the next morning. "She's still alive," said Tracy. "But we think her head injuries have left her blind."

Over the next two weeks, I visited every house along that stretch of road. When my search for the owner proved fruitless, I felt so guilty that I took the unfortunate creature myself.

"She's lucky to have you," said Tracy, handing her over.

So that became her name – Lucky.

## Musings

Guilt is a powerful motivator. Many organizations, especially churches, use guilt to motivate their members. They can make you feel guilty for having sinned, for not giving enough money or time, for doubting their doctrines, or for failing to eliminate injustice and oppression.

But I've learned something from little Lucky. Guilt is useless – unless it prompts you to actually do something about the problem. Guilt needs to turn into involvement.

If I'm going fight injustice, I need to see that my contribution, however big or small, actually makes a difference. It's not enough just to toss my efforts into a huge amorphous pot, like a raindrop falling into the ocean. Then, when I see that I have made a difference, I can replace the enervating emotion of guilt with the more positive emotions of joy, celebration, and solidarity.

Little Lucky did fine, after a while. I was proud of her. She never did regain her sight, but she learned to get around our house without bumping into things or falling down the stairs. She trotted happily along beside my large shoes. She climbed into our laps and purred happily.

If she was lucky, so were we.

---

**Bible reading:** John 19:25–27.
Behold your son.

# Monkeying Around

The woman in the seat beside me on the plane stared as I peeled a banana.

I was flying WestJet. Not serving meals saves WestJet so much money that they can charge several hundred dollars less than Air Canada for the same flight from Kelowna to Toronto. So I take my own lunch along.

"I've never seen anyone peel a banana that way before," my seatmate remarked.

I must have looked surprised.

"From the flower end," she explained. "Everyone I know starts at the stem end."

I explained that I had learned this trick from watching monkeys. Normally, we humans grab the stem end and wrench it back and forth until the tough skin snaps. If it doesn't snap easily, we crush and bruise the fruit underneath.

"Monkeys always peel from the flower end," I said. "It's much easier. It also avoids the necessity of having to eat mashed banana."

Now it was her turn to look surprised. "I never thought of learning anything from a monkey," she said.

## Musings

Where did we get the notion that we can learn only from creatures that are more intelligent than we are?

Of course, when we take courses in school, we expect our teachers to know more than we do. At work, we expect the manager or the floor boss to know the job better than we do. And we hope some of that superior knowledge will transfer to us, like water flowing downhill.

But if we always had to learn from someone who knew more, a real genius would be in deep trouble.

Isaac Newton could not have discovered gravity or invented calculus. Einstein would still be a Swiss patent clerk. Mozart would have had to wait for Beethoven to come along before taking piano lessons.

Take the notion the opposite direction, on the other hand, and you have a more comfortable discovery – we can learn from anything. Which, in fact, we do. Biologists study algae and lichens and learn how those primitive life forms survive conditions that would destroy us.

And we don't have to become lichens or algae to learn from them, any more than we have to become monkeys to learn to peel a banana from the flower end. In the same way, we can learn from all other humans, even when we profoundly disagree with them. Christians don't have to abandon their faith to learn from Muslims or Hindus. Men don't have to become effeminate to learn about emotions and relationships. Heterosexual couples don't have to turn gay – or vice versa – to recognize the virtue of lifelong commitment to a partner.

A writer who belonged to the conservative Christian Reformed Church once commented that the Bible was God's religious textbook, and the world was God's science textbook. I like that idea. It says that I don't have to choose between the two sources. Knowledge and wisdom can come from any source, if I'm willing to receive it.

---

**Bible reading:** Proverbs 6:6–8.
Look to the ant.

# IRRATIONAL REACTIONS

Fear makes people act irrationally. It affects cats that way too.

Our cat is called Mush for two reasons. When you pet her, she goes sort of mushy in your arms. Mush is also what she has between her ears. She doesn't think very much.

I had brought home a plastic grocery bag of small wind-up toys from the thrift shop run by our church. Some of the toys worked, some didn't. I planned to take them apart to see if any of the non-working toys were salvageable. I left the bag on a chair in the den while I did something else.

Mush jumped up onto the chair. She saw the bag, and with the curiosity typical of cats, she poked herself inside to see if there was anything there to play with. She must have touched a toy that was fully wound up, just waiting to spring into noisy action.

Mush exploded out of the bag. Or rather, she tried to explode out of the bag. Unfortunately, she tried to get out through one of the hand holes. She's too big to pass through that hole. So the bag travelled with her.

We didn't see all this, of course. It all happened too fast. Rather, we heard some strange sounds that moved with astonishing speed from our den through the kitchen to the living room. When we followed the sounds, we found a trail of little mechanical toys, buzzing, beeping, squawking, walking, and rotating.

Mush cowered behind the couch, trembling, while the last of the toys unwound itself in the shredded remains of the plastic bag still looped around her neck.

## Musings

It's easy for us humans to rationalize that if Mush had just stayed still, no harm would have come to her, and we could easily have disentangled her from the bag. But panic doesn't work that way, in cats or in humans. People who feel scared or threatened react in unpredictable ways. Some run and hide, like Mush. Others launch personal attacks. It's what's called the "fight or flight" reflex.

The temple priests in Jerusalem crucified the objects of their fears.

Once, while I was witnessing a conflict that was starting to get vicious, I asked the two staff members, "What is it that you're afraid of happening here?" It was an intuitive question. I didn't know what else to ask. But it turned out that when they faced their fears, they were able to realize that their goals were not that far apart after all.

We don't pay enough attention to our fears. We acknowledge other motivations, such as greed, guilt, generosity, altruism, or cynicism. But we don't recognize, or are unwilling to recognize, the extent to which our fears push our buttons.

Even in places that promote compassion and sensitivity, we often react irrationally if we feel threatened. We lash out – at gay ordination or same-sex marriage, at changes to the Sunday morning liturgy, or at portrayals of Jesus as black or physically handicapped.

When we know what we're afraid of, we can act responsibly to deal with it. We don't need to attack others personally.

---

**Bible reading:** 1 John 4:16b–21.
        Perfect love casts out fear.

# IN OUR ELEMENT

A heron surged out of the trees along the lakeshore the other day. It swooped low over the water, long trailing legs almost surfing, wings spread with not a feather twitching. At the last second, it pulled up and landed on top of a weathered piling.

A heron on land is a gawky and ungainly creature. A heron in the air is effortless beauty.

In Africa, a couple of years ago, we saw a number of marabou storks standing around a waterhole. The guidebook described them as "enormous *ugly* birds (the guidebook italicized the word ugly for emphasis) whose long white legs are usually covered with its own excrement." We concurred with that description – on land.

But in the air, they were something quite different.

I watched a mature marabou stork come in for a landing in a thicket of acacia trees. It had a wingspan of close to eight feet. Yet it came gliding in, banking through the branches, with a grace and precision that almost left me in tears.

Penguins on ice are comic figures. Penguins in water are a thing of beauty, a joy to see.

Birds need to be seen in their own element to be fully appreciated.

## Musings

Every creature has its own natural element. Humans are more awkward in water than on land – although technologies like swim fins and air tanks assist us considerably. Unassisted, humans fly about as well as a brick. But even on land, we are less graceful than a cheetah, less agile than a monkey, and less powerful than a horse.

But are land, water, and air the only elements? Could relationship be an element too?

When I was a lot younger, I thought the ideal was to be independent and self-sufficient. To owe nothing to anyone and to be owed nothing by anyone. As I grow older, I sense that such a person would not be fully human. He (or she) would be a caricature, a cardboard cut-out, a dysfunctional figment of cultural misanthropy.

More and more, I believe that we realize our full humanness only in relationship – with each other, with God, with our environments. We most clearly reveal our true selves through the quality of our relationships.

Perhaps relationship is the only thing that humans excel at. Other creatures – wolves and whales come to mind – are also social animals. But none of them, as far as I know, have developed the range of relationships that humans have. All creatures have some sort of family or tribal function. But only humans add the overlapping layers of relationship invoked by politics, science, employment, and recreation, among many other things. And thanks to technology, our relationships are not even restricted to proximity. By e-mail and Internet, I can have friends anywhere in the world.

We are not conscious of this element, just as I'm sure fish are not conscious of the water they swim in. But without relationships, we humans are as lost as a fish out of water.

---

**Bible reading:** Matthew 12:46–50.
Who is my family?

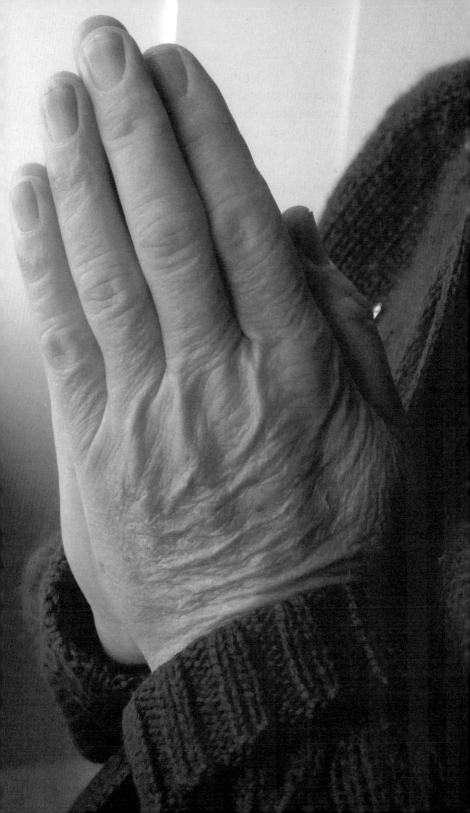

# Praying without Words

Joan and I had just settled down to have lunch at our picnic table outside on the deck. The dog, who had spent most of the morning sprawled on top of an air-conditioning vent trying to keep cool in the height of the summer heat, suddenly decided life was worth living after all. He sauntered up to the table, plunked his jowls on the edge of it, and stared at our sandwiches. If telekinesis had any validity, those sandwiches should have voluntarily slid across the table into his mouth.

I closed my eyes and started to say grace. "For this food, dear God –"

Someone burped. Not a gentle little "excuse me" kind of burp. A rich, rolling, and resonant, "Urrrrrrupppp!"

It was the dog.

I tried to keep a straight face. Joan dissolved in hysterical laughter.

"That probably expresses anticipation of good things to come better than anything I could say," I rationalized.

### Musings

Whether a burp is or is not an acceptable form of grace depends on one's understanding of prayer. If you expect prayer to use well-practised words and phrases, it isn't.

When I was a small child, my bedtime prayers followed an unchanging ritual. I described my day. I said thank you. And I concluded with the same sequence: "God bless Grandpa and Grandma in Canada, and Granny and Grandpa in Ireland, and God bless Mummy and Daddy, and make me a good boy. Amen."

That litany didn't change until my grandparents started dying. The first time I had to leave out

"Grandpa in Ireland," I stumbled to a standstill. I couldn't carry on.

Over the years, I've grown less and less comfortable with routine prayer formulas. They trip too easily off the tongue, or through the mind. One phrase follows another, like beads on a string, without much original thought or room for reflection in between.

Some of my friends like their prayers that way. They tell me that the constant repetition of a *Hail Mary* or similar mantra-like sequence frees their minds to wander, meditate, and hear God whispering within them.

It puts me to sleep. When my mind does wander, it moves in directions that I'm not sure God approves of.

A few years ago, though, I heard a fragment of a radio interview. Almost as an afterthought, the interviewer asked, "What is prayer?"

And the interviewee – I think she might have been a New York playwright – replied, "Prayer is the deepest longing of the heart."

I loved that definition. That kind of prayer doesn't need words. What someone really longs, hungers, and thirsts for will shape every aspect of that person's life. It will express itself in that person's actions and relationships. And, yes, it will affect the words that person uses to express those longings.

So if our dog's burp expressed his deepest longing, it was indeed a prayer.

---

**Bible reading:** 1 Thessalonians 5:12–22.
Pray without ceasing.

# HUMAN ACTIVITIES

By far the greatest number of Jesus' parables deal with human activities. Humans live in societies. For the people of his time – as for ours – the bulk of interactions are with other humans. That's why the majority of Jesus' parables still speak to us.

Our technological environment has changed enormously. I have trouble imagining how hot-headed, bumble-mouthed Simon Peter would deal with modern airport security measures, for example, if he were suddenly transported into the 21st century! Would Mary and Joseph have slept in a stable if they had a 1-800 number to call in advance for reservations?

In spite of technological change, though, our human interactions still remain remarkably unchanged. We still act out of love or hate, fear or trust, greed or generosity. And so the famous parables of the good Samaritan, the sheep and the goats, the prodigal son, and the wedding guests still resonate with our contemporary experience.

Even if today's parables occur in a context that would be totally unfamiliar to biblical readers.

# ACT OF PROTEST

Thirty years ago, an organization called Crossroads Canada recruited me to spend six weeks in Malawi – the poorest country in Africa – to help a consortium of churches there improve their public relations publications.

The largest of those churches – grandly called the Church of Central Africa Presbyterian and founded by Presbyterian missionary and explorer David Livingstone – owned a large piece of valuable property in the country's largest city, Blantyre. For generations, village people heading to the city's central market had crossed that property. The path through the compound had been pounded hard by millions of bare feet.

Then the managers of the church consortium, all of them African, decided to protect the property rights bequeathed to them by their Scottish predecessors. They put up a chain-link fence. Six feet high. Right across the path used by their present-day relatives.

The villagers did not protest. They were not accustomed to demanding their rights. Indeed, they were not accustomed to having rights. They lived in a dictatorship where they did as they were told. So they simply detoured around the fence.

A few of us there (mainly idealistic whites) felt that the villagers had suffered an injustice. Sometimes, as we sat in dimly lit living rooms while geckos chased insects around the walls above our heads, we talked about restoring the villagers' traditional right of way.

The governing council of managers had already rejected an appeal from my host, Tom Colvin. (Tom is now dead, so I can tell this story.)

On my last night in his house, I said, "Tom, there's one more thing I need to do before I leave."

"What's that?" he asked.

"I need to borrow a pair of pliers, with wire cutters."

"I'll come with you," he said.

"No," I replied. "If I do it myself, I'll be out of the country before anyone discovers it, and no one can blame anyone who's still here."

"I'll come with you," he repeated.

In the pitch black of an equatorial night, we snipped through the wire of the fence. We unwound the interlocked links. We opened a hole in the fence. We pushed the chain back on both sides of the old path. The next morning I flew out of Malawi.

A few weeks later, I received a letter from Tom Colvin. "The local people were using the old path by the very next morning," he wrote delightedly. "The managers held an emergency meeting to decide what to do about this act of malicious vandalism. In the end, they left the hole in the fence open. They decided that historic rights mattered more than property rights!"

To this day, part of me worries that what I did that night was wrong. In our Western culture, property rights tend to take priority over human rights. I had "trespassed," both literally, and as the term is used in the Lord's Prayer. I had damaged physical property.

Another part of me still believes that what I did was right. Instead of sitting passively by, watching an injustice take place, I had acted. I had obeyed my conscience.

## Musings

I had choices that night. I could have left things as they were. No one would have criticized me for failing to get involved. Or I could get involved in an act that violated one set of social standards in favour of another set of standards. Under Malawi's laws, it might even have been classed as a criminal offence.

I made a choice.

I don't regret it.

**Bible reading:** Deuteronomy 30:15–20a.
Choose life.

# Adversarial Systems

It's astonishing, sometimes, how informal the lower courts can be. The judge, the prosecutor, and the clerk casually discuss how to move the various cases through most fairly.

"Oops," said the prosecutor at a traffic court in Toronto, as he noted an error in the charges. "I think we'll have to throw this one out."

The judge nodded. There was no attempt to pursue a conviction regardless; the bemused defendant didn't need a defence lawyer to enter a motion for dismissal.

In an Edmonton court, half a dozen persons failed to appear. "I suppose we have to issue warrants," the judge sighed.

It was nothing like television. There was no ruthless cross examination, à la Perry Mason; no legal wrangling, as in *Law & Order*; no highly technical evidence, as in the various *CSI* clones. If anything, it felt more like *Night Court*, without the laugh track.

Periodically, the crown prosecutor took people aside to discuss the charges against them, and to consider alternatives for their plea.

One young man elected to stand trial immediately, rather than wait for a later date. He chose to defend himself. The judge carefully explained the procedures. And aside from two minutes while he took the stand himself, mostly to complain that he had been unfairly treated, the defendant spent the trial slouched in his chair, looking for all the world like Zonker in the *Doonesbury* cartoon strip.

The judge asked the young man if he was ready for sentencing.

"It don't matter," the man mumbled without rising. "I don't got no money to pay your fine, and I don't got no job neither."

"How long would you need to raise the money?" the judge asked. "Six months? I can specify whatever would work for you."

The defendant just shrugged. "Whatever…" he muttered. He didn't seem impressed that the judge was trying to help him.

## Musings

It must be depressing for the judges to have a constant parade of bewildered, mildly paranoid, or utterly incompetent people passing through a court.

A former classmate, now a lawyer, told me once that family court officials watch for the four R's – *Revenge, Recrimination, Retribution,* and *Retaliation.* Even in relatively amicable negotiated separations, he said, the four R's almost always show up eventually. Some lawyers literally tick them off as they emerge.

As one who lives with words, I wondered why some other R words don't occur – words like *Remorse, Reconciliation, Renewal,* even *Resurrection.*

"Not likely," said my friend. "By the time you get to court, you're into an adversarial system. For one party to win, the other has to lose."

I'd go further and say that in any adversarial system, both parties lose. In a contested divorce, everyone loses something, especially any children. No one wins a war; one side simply loses less than the other side.

But my limited experience suggests that it is possible for the professional members of a court to minimize the disadvantages of an adversarial system and make it more humane for all concerned. They can treat people as something more than widgets on an assembly line. A little consultation, a little listening, a little flexibility – these things can go a long way to mitigate the sense of being unfairly picked on.

---

**Bible reading:** Luke 13:1–9.
A second chance, not punishment.

# SHADES OF HUMAN NATURE

The 1982 Jaguar XJ6 sedan is a gorgeous car. Some call it Sir William Lyons' most beautiful design. I bought one in 1998. It was already 16 years old. The odometer had been around at least twice.

Over the next few years, I spent about $14,000 restoring the body and rebuilding the engine and transmission. But it wasn't enough: rust started to bubble under my lovely new paintwork; the leather upholstery cracked and split; electrical components died unpredictably. And I knew I wouldn't spend the additional money the car needed because I had been seduced by a newer Jaguar.

For most of a year, I advertised the older car for sale without success. I lowered my price progressively from $10,000 to $3,000. Only two people even inquired. Neither of them bought the car.

I concluded that the car was doing no one any good rusting in my driveway, so I ran an ad in the newspaper, offering to give my car away free to a good home.

I got deluged with calls. My answering machine overloaded. In the first two days, I responded to over 100 calls. I told the callers that I would decide who got the car within two days and would let them know.

When I called them back, I got three kinds of reactions: grateful, casual, and hostile.

The first group, I realized, were those who really cared about the car itself, and hoped to make it once more a thing of a beauty and a joy to drive. They regretted not getting the car themselves, but they were glad it had gone to someone with a proven record of restoring cars.

The second group simply needed a car (for a variety of heart-tugging reasons). They didn't care what it was, as long as it didn't cost them anything. This group rarely thanked me for calling them back. Most, I suspect, wondered why I had bothered calling them at all if they didn't get the car.

The third group, the hostile ones, thought they were entitled to this car because I had offered to give it away. Fortunately they were very few. They responded to my call with anger. I had taken away something that they assumed was already theirs. They screamed that my offer was a cruel hoax, that I didn't play fair, or that I had lied to them.

It was an interesting exposure to human nature.

## Musings

The three different reactions seem to me to illustrate a broader pattern of human response.

For some people, the cause, the goal, the purpose, matters. They're willing to make sacrifices to further that cause. They're the ones who make a difference.

A few believe the world owes them a living. They feel entitled to whatever they want.

Fortunately for all of us, this group is a small minority.

In between lies the second group, by far the largest. They see life for what they can get out of it, and what it provides for them. They're not dangerous, but neither are they helpful in building a better world.

Every one of us probably belongs to each of these three groups at various times, depending on circumstances. It takes a specific incident, such as the possibility of getting a free car, to sort out which of the three groups a person falls into. But so do many other commonplace situations – political, social, economic...

How we respond to those situations affects not only ourselves, but also others. A quotation attributed to Edmund Burke says, "The hottest fires in hell are reserved for those who remain neutral in times of moral crisis."

We need to be wary of extremists of any stripe, on the right or on the left. But perhaps we need to be even more careful that we are not encouraging extremists by declining to take a stand ourselves.

Burke is probably better known for another quotation: "All that's necessary for the forces of evil to win in the world is for enough good men to do nothing."

**Bible reading:**  Revelation 3:1b–2, 15–17.
Neither hot nor cold.

# Rescuing Lost Logs

A big wind roared up the 135-kilometre length of Okanagan Lake one night. With nothing obstructing it, the storm generated a lot of power before it encountered the log booms tethered on the west side of the lake. It ripped the booms from their moorings.

The morning after the storm, I took the dog for her usual walk along the lakeshore. All along the shore, extending farther out than I could possibly throw a rock, a carpet of logs rocked gently on the water. There were hundreds of bundles, each one comprising a whole truckload of logs lashed together.

"There must be 500–600 bundles loose along here," sighed an employee of the logging company as he stared out at his company's property.

Later in the afternoon, company boats arrived to collect the loose bundles. They drove their boats the way cowboys drive horses. They circled the straying bundles, rounding them up. They herded the gathered bundles together in a sheltered cove. They raced to head off errant bundles of logs drifting farther along the lake. They lassoed loose logs and dragged them home.

It took them three days to rescue every lost log.

## Musings

Why, I wonder, do we in churches cling so single-minded-ly to the biblical metaphor of shepherd? The shepherd who leaves the ninety-and-nine to go after the one lost sheep. The shepherd who leads his flock to still waters and green pastures. The "Good Shepherd." In almost 60 years of attending church, I can't begin to count the number of sermons and children's stories I've heard that use the metaphors of sheep and shepherds.

But very few of us know any sheep personally.

The first time we took our daughter Sharon to Ireland, she looked out the car window one dreary day

when the rain lashed horizontally across emerald fields, and asked: "Dad, what are those fuzzy-looking rocks out there?"

Just then one of the "rocks" got up and shook itself. "They're sheep," I explained.

Sharon went into paroxysms of laughter. I never did find out what she expected sheep to look like, but it certainly wasn't fuzzy rocks. In that brief exchange, though, I realized how meaningless a central image of the Bible must be to her. If she didn't know anything at all about sheep, how was she to understand Jesus' parables about sheep? How could she comprehend, "The Lord is my shepherd..."?

Shepherding has become a second-hand experience. We know it only by hearsay. We know something *about* it. But it's not something we recognize ourselves actually *doing*.

And yet there's shepherding going on constantly, all around us. Kindergarten teachers shepherd their pupils across a busy intersection. Ushers shepherd theatre patrons to their proper seats. School bus drivers shepherd rambunctious teenagers safely to their destination. Mothers gather their youngsters around them on a trip to the shopping mall, making sure none of the flock get lost. Air traffic controllers shepherd airliners full of passengers through distant skies to the safety of a runway. Firefighters, avalanche rescue workers, paramedics, and cops leave the main flock in safety while they rescue the lost and missing. Doctors, nurses, psychiatrists, and therapists nurse injured patients back to health.

When we restrict our relationship with God by clinging to an archaic rural metaphor, we deny ourselves the privilege of seeing God at work in dozens of ways every day.

**Bible reading:** John 21:15–17.
Passing on the Shepherd's role.

# MEETINGS AND MORE MEETINGS

I woke up one morning dreading the day ahead.

I had an appointment for a meeting at 9:30 a.m., at 1:00 p.m. with another immediately following, and a fourth at 6:30 that night.

And I found myself wondering, "Is this what I retired for?"

Corporate executives might consider four meetings an easy day. Cabinet ministers who have to read briefing notes as they rush from meeting to meeting might actually welcome a day with only four meetings. But it was not my idea of heaven.

Omar Khayyám thought heaven consisted of leisure and luxury:

> *A jug of wine, a loaf of bread, and thou*
> *beside me singing in the wilderness...*

I don't share Omar Khayyám's delight in sheer idleness. But at the same time, I resent bouncing like a billiard ball from appointment to appointment.

I tolerate meetings better than I once did. I used to consider all meetings a waste of time, a way of avoiding actually doing the work that the meeting was supposed to facilitate. Today, I'm more inclined to see meetings as their own justification – a primitive form of mass communication through which participants slowly evolve towards a collective vision. The work eventually achieved – I'm still an optimist! – will differ from the work that would have been done if those meetings had never happened.

But I'd much rather just get on with doing the work.

## Musings

I resent meetings. But I go to them. Not because I expect to accomplish anything there, and certainly not because meetings attract me. Egotistically, I suppose I go because I'm afraid that the other members might make a ghastly mistake without me. More likely, I go because I don't want to let friends and colleagues down. I've been to meetings that no one wanted to attend. Every one of us had more important things to do. But we didn't feel we could disappoint the others, so we went.

A few months before his death, I called my friend Peter Honor. "He's watching a soccer game on TV with Andrew because he thinks Andrew wants to watch it with him," his wife Carolynn told me.

"I didn't think Andrew was a soccer fan," I said.

"He's not," she replied. "He's watching soccer because he thinks Peter wants him to watch it with him."

It's the loss of personal autonomy that irritates me most. A meeting expects me, even requires me, to attend at a predetermined time and place, whether it happens to be convenient or not.

Long ago, only kings and prelates had the power to call people together. Otherwise, people met on the job, on the road, or in the pub. Discussions that happened during casual encounters flowered into consensus. Business got done. And people got on with life.

Today, anyone can call a meeting at any time. I'm not sure that's progress.

I skipped my last meeting that day. Instead, I stayed home and wrote this story.

---

**Bible reading:** Matthew 18:15–20.
Gathering people for a purpose.

# HOMELY RESURRECTIONS

Joan was away for a week. While she was gone, the house and I suffered through the missing-spouse syndrome. It could also be called the bachelor syndrome, except that it doesn't apply only to bachelors. Any male, left to fend for himself, seems to go through this process. And I don't mean just not having meals prepared. I'm quite capable of boiling eggs and ordering pizza, thank you.

The morning Joan left, the house was spotless.

By noon, there were dirty dishes stacked in the sink.

By that evening, there were tea stains on the counters, the bed was still un-made, and the kitty litter reeked.

By the second morning, the milk in the jug I had forgetfully left on the counter had gone sour, and my deodorant stick ran out.

That evening, I tripped over the pyjamas I had left lying on the floor.

By the third morning, I couldn't use the dining table for the newspapers littered over it, and the toilet paper roll in the bathroom needed replacing.

The house, I thought, had begun a descent into hell.

## Musings

The phrase "descended into hell" comes fairly readily to my tongue. I have repeated it countless times in reciting the Apostles' Creed, which asserts that Jesus "descended into hell; on the third day he rose again from the dead."

Some may feel that it is trivializing at best, blasphemous at worst, to use the same description for a dirty house as for the resurrection of the Christ. But that depends on one's view of the resurrection. With or without a capital R.

For those who see the resurrection as a one-time-only intervention into history that overturns all the normal rules of nature, then relating it to the progressive chaos of a home-alone husband is indeed trivializing. I respect that view. But I do not hold it. Because if we take the view that Christ's resurrection was intended to remind us of the renewals that occur constantly in our lives, then I am not trivializing at all in describing disorder in a home. Rather, the resurrection becomes the most dramatic symbol possible for drawing our attention to recurring patterns that we too easily overlook.

I believe we are constantly resurrected. Not from physical death, admittedly. But from many lesser deaths – the death of a dream, a relationship, an ability, a project... When the predictable equilibrium of life shatters like a dropped wineglass, we are for a time destroyed by that loss. And then, by the grace of God, we bounce back – not the same as we were, but still recognizably ourselves.

By this view, an ending is never just an ending, but also a beginning.

And so, after Joan had been away for about three days, I found myself cleaning up. Washing the dishes. Wiping the counters. Replacing the toilet paper. By the time she returned home, the house had had its own resurrection.

And, I suppose, so had I.

---

**Bible reading:** 1 Corinthians 15:12–20.
Raised from the dead.

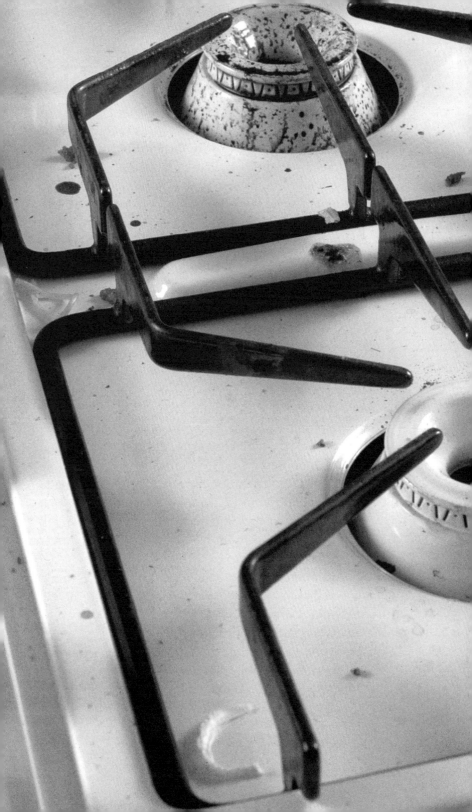

# OUR HEAVENLY GRANDPARENT

Something about being a grandparent turns rational and literate persons into babbling clowns. Either they babble *to* the grandchild, or they babble *about* the grandchild.

One acquaintance kept a gold box on the coffee table in his living room. The lid bore the cryptic initials **H Y S M A G**. I couldn't figure out what they meant. After a few visits, I mustered the courage to ask what the initials stood for.

"I'm so glad you asked," he replied. "*Have You Seen My Adorable Grandchildren?*"

The box was filled with photos of his grandkids, which he proceeded to show me. For almost an hour.

Joan and I came late to grandparenting. Many of our friends achieved that status much earlier. In the past, as I've watched our friends' critical faculties dissolve into mush where their grandchildren are concerned, I have wondered what could cause such a personality change.

Now I'm doing it myself.

I realized it had happened to me too the first time I rocked my granddaughter, Katherine Rediet Taylor, in my arms one pearly-early morning in Ethiopia. I cooed. I gurgled. I made silly faces. I recalled the words of songs that I had not sung for 40 years, nursery rhymes that my mother probably sang to me when I was Katherine's age.

Katherine has very dark irises. Those big dark eyes gazed up at me. Although I had no idea what she might be thinking, I knew in that moment that she depended totally on me. And I knew that I must respond. I cannot betray that trust. All that matters is making her happy.

And when she smiles at me, my heart does flip-flops.

Technically, tiny Katherine is not even related to me. That doesn't matter. My brain has turned to mush.

## Musings

It must have something to do with the utter vulnerability of infants. They cannot take matters into their own hands. They have to trust this person holding them. And we – most of us, anyway – reciprocate. We don't enter into this relationship with suspicion, wondering what hidden agendas this person might have, what they're trying to sell us, or what benefit we might derive from this relationship.

We simply enter into that relationship, without imposing conditions upon it.

Jesus talked about little children. "Unless you can become like a little child," he told the crowd gathered around him, "you can never enter God's heaven." We usually assume he was talking about children old enough to run around, play, learn, and interact with him. But it could just as easily have been babies that mothers brought to him, hoping he would bless them.

Suppose it was a newborn he took in his arms. "Unless you become as vulnerable and trusting as this infant," he might have said, "you will never experience the depth of God's love."

Maybe, like his disciples, we humans try too hard to earn God's love. We want to be worthy. Maybe we even want to interact with God as equals. But in reality, we can't really carry on an intelligent conversation with God. At least, I can't. If nothing else, God's time frame differs from mine. If a thousand years is like a day in God's time, how could I possibly identify individual words?

But maybe I don't have to. Maybe God is happy when I quit struggling, when I lie back in those "everlasting arms," when I let God coo and gurgle delightedly over me.

---

**Bible reading:** Mark 10:13–16.
Like a little child.

# THE ULTIMATE AUDIENCE

One year, Joan and I took our winter holiday in Cozumel, the island in the Caribbean just off the coast of Mexico's Yucatan peninsula. Most evenings, we went into the island's only town, San Miguel, for dinner.

Among the restaurants of San Miguel, bananas flambé was a competitive sport.

Whenever we ordered a flambé dessert, ordinary waiters cleared out. The headwaiter in black jacket showed up with a cart of magician's tools. He cooked the bananas in syrup beside our table. When they were sizzling, he peeled a fresh orange so that its skin hung down in a long spiral. Then he carefully poured the brandy down the spiral of peel. As it ran into the scorching hot griddle, the liquor burst into flame and fire raced up the spiral of orange peel to the top.

The restaurant patrons always burst into applause.

The performance had little effect on the taste of the bananas. But the headwaiter usually got a fat tip.

In much the same way, the best Spanish coffee I recall having was in a restaurant in a converted water mill in the small town of Elora, northwest of Toronto. Again, the performance made the difference. The waiter didn't just bring a mug of prepared coffee steaming from the kitchen. He prepared it beside our table – heating the glass, rolling the rim in sugar, adding the liquor, the coffee, the whipped cream, and the cinnamon. We were salivating long before the drinks touched our table.

We were an appreciative audience.

## Musings

So who's the audience for our life performances?

Because life has to be more than just a momentary flicker on the serial drama of reality. As one of

Peggy Lee's songs commented: "If that's all there is...let's break out the booze, and have a ball."

If life is "but a fleeting shadow, a poor player that struts and frets his hour upon the stage" (Shakespeare, if you hadn't already recognized the quotation), why would we bother with such trivial matters as honesty, loyalty, friendship, or love? If this is all there is, why not get what you can while you can? You're not going to be around to pay for it later.

Yet surely we are not just consumers who expect to be entertained by the world around us. We are also the performers. And we make a difference, for good or for ill. Every time we mess up one of our scenes, we affect other performances. Other people's performances. Even the performance of the earth itself.

I've heard it said that when people gather in a church to worship, the minister is not the performer, nor the congregation the audience. Rather, the congregation is the performer and God the audience.

But why limit that principle to a weekly hour of worship? If there is a God, isn't it reasonable to assume that God observes the whole of life? If so, what kind of performance does God see each of us put on?

---

**Bible reading:** Psalm 139:1–6.
Known intimately.

# DOING THINGS DIFFERENTLY

Coffee does not get along with me. I drink it only in emergencies. For years, I blamed coffee for causing heartburn that was eventually diagnosed as acid reflux. So I have been known to protest when a church's after-service "coffee time" provides nothing but coffee.

I prefer tea. I have drunk tea from Darjeeling, Ceylon, China, and Malaysia. I have had black tea, spiced tea, green tea, jasmine tea, and even gunpowder tea. My mother taught me to use water at a rolling boil, pre-heat the teapot, and steep the tea for seven minutes.

But the very best tea I ever tasted violated all the conventional rules about making good tea.

I was a university student, on a summer job in the forests inland from Kitimat on the north coast of British Columbia. Bob Williamson and I had spent six weeks slogging up and down the canyon of the Kitimat River, tallying the timber resources.

That night, I remember, we camped beside a burbling stream, clear as ice and twice as cold. For the first time in weeks, we had moved beyond the steep walls of the valley carved by the river. Wide blue skies opened out above us. As we cooked our supper, the rays of the setting sun shone into our campsite and warmed us.

I started to make tea.

"Here, let me do that," said Willi.

He scooped fresh water from the stream, threw some nondescript tea leaves loose into the cold water, and perched the pot over our campfire.

"Cold water?" I protested.

"Wait and see," he assured me.

He never did let the water boil. When it started to bubble around the edges of the pot, he pulled the pot off the fire and poured the amber liquid into our cups.

I have never tasted better tea. The setting, and a hard day's work, might have influenced my perceptions. But I still think I have never drunk better tea.

## Musings

Many of us take for granted that the English way of making tea is the only way. Yet just how does a nation whose culinary reputation is based on bangers and mash dictate the proper procedures for making tea? That's not how they make tea in India, Ceylon, or China – the original tea-drinking nations. In the same way, I suggest, we take for granted many religious teachings. We absorbed them back in Sunday school, and have never questioned them since.

A few years ago, the moderator of the United Church of Canada shocked many people when he admitted that he had questions about the common belief that Jesus was directly fathered by God. People reacted as though this was heresy. Unthinkable. Why?

To my mind, there is only one reason for refusing to consider something new – be it an idea or an experience. Could it hurt me? Could it hurt someone else?

Perhaps we fear anything new because it upsets our applecart. It might cause us to rethink things we have long taken for granted. I suspect we're more likely to be harmed by things that we refuse to consider (even if we ultimately reject them) than by new ideas that we do consider.

---

**Bible reading:** Isaiah 43:18–19.
God does a new thing.

# BIG ROCKS FIRST

Not all parables are stories. Some are demonstrations.

I've used this enacted parable a couple of times with groups. First I take a big enamel pot or a big glass jar. Carefully, I fill it with fist-sized rocks until I can't get any more in.

"Is it full?" I ask the members of the group.

Yes it is, they agree. So I pour in a bag of gravel. It fills the gaps between the rocks. I fill the container right to the top again.

"Now is it full?" I ask.

Yes it is, they agree. So I start pouring in fine dry sand. It spills down through the gravel, filling up all the spaces.

"Now is it full?" I ask.

Yes, they agree, it certainly is.

So I take a jug of water, and start pouring. And pouring. It's amazing how much water will go in, when I've already filled the pot with rock, gravel, and sand.

"Now is it full?" I ask.

By now they're beginning to get the idea. They wonder what else I could add. Sugar, perhaps; that would dissolve in the water. Gases. Food colouring.

"So what's the moral of this parable?" I ask.

Someone always says, "No matter how busy you are, you can always squeeze in something more." And everyone nods. They see it as an exhortation to do more, to put more stress into their lives.

I shake my head. "You missed the first point," I say. "If you don't get the big rocks in first, you'll never get them in at all."

## Musings

It's a sobering demonstration for most of us. Because when we get pushed, it's often the "big rocks" in our lives, the really important things that make us what we are, that get set aside.

We won't all share the same "big rocks." Some people need security for survival; others need risk. Few of us will even have the same "big rocks" consistently throughout our lives. When I was 30, my career mattered most. Today, it's my relationships – with my wife, my daughter, my friends, my grandchildren. Ten years from now, it may be my health.

We don't all have to have the same big rocks. But we all have to make room for those big rocks, or we become tumbleweeds blown around by every breeze. We have to know what our "big rocks" are, to make sure they're there.

One of the most overlooked "rocks," in my opinion, is faith. Not faith in the sense of having a set of doctrines to affirm. But faith as that deep underlying conviction that life has some purpose, some meaning. Various cultures express that faith in various ways. Some proclaim one God; some proclaim many gods; at least one proclaims no god at all. But they all provide a framework for life that connects us to a larger purpose.

Without that, nothing we do has much meaning. We become a jar filled with nothing but shifting sand.

---

**Bible reading:** 1 Corinthians 13:1–4.
If I do not have love, I am nothing.

# Living with Ambiguity

Like many married couples, when Joan and I are out together, I usually drive; she navigates. Most of the time that division of labour works fairly well. But sometimes it doesn't.

One night, I remember, we were going for dinner at a restaurant on the far side of the city. It was in an area unfamiliar to me, although Joan knew it fairly well. So I had to depend on her directions.

"Turn right at the church on the corner," she said.

I did. A few blocks farther along, a stop sign appeared in the headlights' glare.

"You can turn left here if you want," said Joan.

I flipped on the left turn flasher and braked to a stop.

"Or you can go straight ahead."

I flipped off the flasher.

"So which way should I go?" I asked.

"That's up to you," she replied.

A car pulled up behind me. Its headlights shone in my rearview mirror.

"How can I decide which way to go when I don't know where the roads go?" I demanded.

Now there were two cars waiting behind me. One of them impatiently flashed his headlights at me.

"Oh, for heaven's sake, go straight on!" she spluttered.

"Thank you," I said (with a trace of sarcasm, I regret). "That's what I needed to know."

## Musings

Most of the time – in church, for example – I prefer not to have anyone else to do my thinking for me. When Ralph Milton and I founded Wood Lake Books, way back in 1981, we described the first books we published as "religion that doesn't ask you to park your brains at the door."

At the time, Canadian religious publishing was dormant or worse. Ryerson Press, the United Church's publishing house, had folded in 1971. The Anglican Book Centre produced only what it could persuade Seabury Press to co-publish in the United States. Most books on religious faith came from American televangelists who had their own direct hotline to God, and told their readers exactly what to think.

I resented that.

Getting my faith in gift-wrapped packages is like having someone else do my fitness exercises for me. My faith has to belong to me, not to someone else. So I resent receiving predigested answers to my questions. I'd rather get tough questions that will challenge my easy answers. I want preaching and study that make me think, that invite me to explore my own way through options and possibilities.

Except when I'm driving, of course.

Driving is one of those times when I don't want choices. I want clear, decisive instructions. Don't leave me fumbling with ambiguity when I come to a fork in the road!

So I can understand why the more "conservative" or "evangelical" churches appeal to many people. If you don't know where you're going, if you don't know where your choices might lead you, you want some clear directions. Not multiple options.

---

**Bible reading:**  Matthew 7:13–14.
Entry by the narrow gate.

# Encountering the Holy

On a dismal, rainy afternoon in Ireland, Joan and I were visiting my cousin David's cottage in Donegal. David, however, wasn't there. He had died the year before of a brain tumour.

"Would you like to go for a drive?" asked Isobel, David's widow.

The rain sliced horizontally through the bracken and brambles. It battered the windows. I could barely see past the end of the postage-stamp lawn David had carved out of the rocky hillside.

Inside, a peat fire glowed in the fireplace. An easy chair beckoned.

I almost said no. But Isobel seemed so hopeful.

We drove north, up the inlet, past spectacular red sand beaches to a bay open to the wild North Atlantic. The rain had stopped now, but a bitter wind still drove clouds so low over our heads we could almost reach up and touch them. As the ocean waves rolled in, they curled over slowly, evenly, the crash of foam starting at one end and running steadily across the full width of the bay as each wave in turn exhausted itself on the beach.

Isobel parked her car. We walked out over the dunes to the edge of the beach, leaning into the wind.

"This was David's favourite beach," Isobel said. "He used to come here whenever he could, to go surfing."

For a while, I watched the waves with her, mesmerized by their unceasing rhythm. Then I could stand the wind no longer, and retreated to the shelter of her car. I left Isobel standing on the edge of a dune, knee deep in dune grass, staring out to sea. I had a strange feeling that she could still see David in his wet suit, carving arcs across the face of the waves.

## Musings

I suspect that Isobel came to this beach as a kind of pilgrimage. It was more than nostalgia, more than an attempt to recall a happier past. Because it hurt to come here. It would be so much easier to forget, to bury the past under a welter of routine activities.

But she kept coming back, because this was a holy place for her.

Not because someone had said so. Not because someone had built a shrine. But holy because David had loved this place and she still loved David.

Holiness cannot be imposed externally. I've been to shrines where the piety was laid on so thickly that my primary urge was to laugh, or throw up. I've been to Israel, where there are so many "holy places" that they become boring, even irritating.

Rather, we make places holy by the reverence, the awe, and the empty ache that we bring to them. We come in love; we hope for healing.

The Bible doesn't tell us what Jesus' face looked like after his resurrection. But it does tell us that after Moses had talked with God, his face shone. When Isobel finally returned to the car, her face was shining too. And I don't think it was entirely an effect of the wind.

---

**Bible reading:** Exodus 34:27–30.
Moses' face shines from
encountering God.

# MISCELLANEOUS PARABLES

*There are things that Jesus could not have told parables about because they hadn't happened yet. Christmas, for example. The Romans kept meticulous records of many things, but they never bothered to keep track of the births of Jewish peasant children. And so there is nothing to tell us exactly when Jesus was born. Indeed, analysis of ancient documents suggests that the Christian church did not begin to celebrate Jesus' birth until over three centuries had passed.*

*Yet Christmas has become almost a universal festival in our time. It combines traditions from at least a dozen different countries and cultures. Other faiths even join in the feasting and gift-giving. In our time, it's almost impossible to escape the presence of Christmas.*

*So why not have a parable or two about Christmas?*

*Similarly, Jesus would not have told any parables about skateboards or bicycles, or electricity or railroad trains. If he had, who would have understood him?*

*But they too are part of our lives. Soooooo...*

# THE WORDS DON'T MATTER

Preparations for Christmas, just a week away, turned the normal routines in our home into something midway between anarchy and chaos. So I thought I should explain the rationale for Christmas to my dog Brick.

He gave me his undivided attention, his big brown Irish setter eyes fixed steadily on my face.

I described the concept of the Incarnation. Most Christians believe that Jesus was more than just a good person. By becoming one of us, God validated the human condition – even dying miserably, as most humans still do. But he also showed us that death is not necessarily the end.

Brick's unblinking eyes suggested that he hadn't understood a word.

So I tried reading him the Christmas story, from Matthew's gospel. About the astronomers – or astrologers; there wasn't much difference back then – from a distant eastern nation who followed a star to visit an infant born to an unmarried couple...

Brick just gazed adoringly at me.

I tried Luke's gospel. I read about an angel telling Mary that she would get pregnant, without human assistance, and that her child would be the Son of God. But her baby was born in a smelly stable in a town where she knew nobody. Angels sang in the sky and shepherds stomped through the streets seeking peace and goodwill...

Brick still stared at me without any sign that he had understood the importance of what I had read.

I switched to Santa Claus. I described the original Saint Nicholas, a bishop in Turkey who distributed money to the poor. And how legends evolved until now Santa lives at the North Pole, distributes gifts to children all around the world, and flies through the air in a sleigh pulled by reindeer...

Brick perked up a little when I mentioned reindeer. He usually barks when deer prance through our yard.

I talked about Christmas as a secular celebration. About shopping for presents, sneaking them home, wrapping them up and tucking them under the tree. About the joy of seeing someone's face light up, and knowing that I had found the right gift to express my feelings.

"And we usually put something under the tree for you, too," I assured him.

He slurped a large pink tongue around his jowls, and lay down. I sat beside him on the carpet.

At Christmas, I tried to explain, people renew relationships. They send cards and letters to people that they might never see during the year, to keep in touch. Families gather together. They tell stories and swap jokes and feast on turkey and cranberry sauce, and when they run out of things to say, they sit together companionably and watch Christmas specials on TV...

Those big brown eyes still stared into mine.

I tried to explain that Christmas symbolizes the coming of love into the world. It's a time when we try to treat everyone with the same tenderness we give little babies.

His eyes never changed. So I gave him a hug.

With a deep sigh of contentment, he rested his head in my lap and closed his eyes.

## Musings

Maybe Brick does understand the spirit of Christmas after all.

I wonder why I get so hung up on theology and history, gifts, and legends. Maybe, as the Beatles sang, "All you need is love."

**Bible reading:** 1 Corinthians 13:1–7.
If I do not have love.

# Restoring the Original

Rembrandt's famed painting *Night Watch* hangs in the Rijksmuseum in Amsterdam. Up close, you can find a small patch of lighter, brighter colours in the gloom. A sign informs you that these are Rembrandt's original colours.

Rembrandt, it turns out, did not originally paint a night scene at all. The dark moody colours result from well-intentioned attempts to protect the painting by varnishing it.

Similar things have happened to other great paintings. French inventor Pascal Cotte used infrared and ultraviolet cameras to penetrate the paint layers under the surface of the *Mona Lisa*. He found that in his first version of the world's most famous painting, Leonardo da Vinci's model had eyebrows and lashes; her face was wider and her smile more expressive.

Cotte then turned his cameras on da Vinci's 1490 *Lady with Ermine*. He discovered that overzealous "improvers" had repainted da Vinci's original blue-grey background with solid black. The black "grossly disfigures the painting," according to Jacques Franck, art historian at UCLA. Cotte's infrared and ultraviolet camera scans also revealed more vivid colours in the Lady's lavish red-and-blue dress, and warmer contours to her flesh.

So now the question becomes – should these paintings be restored to their original vision? Or should they be left as we have come to know them? If an archaeologist found the Venus de Milo's missing arms, should they be glued back on? Or should she remain as we have admired her for so long?

Some art experts fear that Cotte's discoveries could inspire ruinous attempts to remove later accretions from old masterpieces.

One side will argue, "Art should be seen as the artist originally envisioned it!"

The other side will reply, "This is the form we have come to know and love. It inspires us as it is. It has become part of our culture. We must not change it."

## Musings

The art world is starting to go through the same discussion that has wracked the religious world for several centuries. Exactly the same arguments have torn religious scholarship.

As scriptures were copied by hand over the centuries, variations crept in. As they were translated from language to language, interpretations crept in. Just like the retouching on paintings. Islam solved the translation problem by decreeing that the Qur'an is authoritative only in Arabic, although that doesn't eliminate the risk of narrow interpretations.

The best known English version of the Bible is the King James Version, a 1611 translation by committee. However, during the last century, scholars have re-translated the Bible from texts that were not available to the King James committee. They've tried to bring the historic picture out from behind the accumulated varnish of centuries. By translating original Greek and Hebrew texts into the brighter colours of contemporary language, they have tried to restore the vigour and vitality of the original. The scholars of the Jesus Seminar[1] have even tried to define which brush strokes came from Jesus himself, and which were touched up by later assistants.

But many traditionalists insist that it doesn't matter what the originals said. The text as it has come down to us has inspired billions of Christians, and to correct and enhance it, even with the best of intentions, could destroy people's faith.

---

[1] Wikipedia describes the Jesus Seminar as "a group of about 150 individuals, including scholars with advanced degrees in biblical studies...founded in 1985 by the late Robert Funk and John Dominic Crossan...The seminar uses votes with coloured beads to decide their collective view of the historicity of Jesus, specifically what he may or may not have said and done as a historical figure."

The theological world remains split on this issue. I don't expect the art world to achieve consensus quickly either.

---

**Bible reading:** Matthew 5:21–22, 27–28, 31–34a, 38–41. You have heard it said, but I say...

# STACKING CHAIRS

The potluck dinner had ended, the plates had been cleared, and the members were stacking the folding chairs to clear the floor. The chairs looked as if they were all similar. But they weren't. They didn't quite fit together.

They would fit together if you jammed them down. But that tended to damage the edges of the moulded plywood seats, which in turn tended to leave splinters in the next user's posterior.

"No, no, not like that," instructed a long-time member. "You have to match the colours!"

Superficially, the chairs all looked the same – plywood seats, plywood backs, and metal frames.

"Look at the colour of the frames," explained the organizer. "Put the brown frames with the brown frames, the grey frames with the grey, and so on."

With that change, the chairs stacked together perfectly.

## Musings

We have an ideal that religious people should get along with each other. They should swallow their disagreements. They should tolerate, even celebrate, their differences. They should set a model for the world on how to get along together. But the ideal doesn't always work. People do have differences. They come from different religious and cultural traditions. They have different ways of working together.

And people would rather hang with those who share similar views than with those who don't.

It's like those stacking chairs.

Superficially, all Christians may look alike. Theoretically, we share the same theology. But I would be seriously unhappy in a fundamentalist congregation.

I would probably be even less happy in a church that called itself The Ultimate Messianic Church of Divine Jesus Christ of the Original Bible. Similarly, a Pentecostal would probably find the worship services I attend much too repressed emotionally. And a Quaker would find them far too noisy.

That doesn't make any of these variations wrong (although I might question the scholarship of the Original Bible people!) but it does suggest that an attempt to homogenize all tastes will have about as much appeal as a four-course turkey dinner put through a blender. The "lowest common denominator" approach satisfies no one.

I'm not suggesting that we exclude those who may look different, or act differently, or come from different backgrounds. Like the shock treatment administered to cardiac arrest victims, a stranger may provide precisely the spark that's needed to revitalize a congregation stalled in the doldrums of deadly routine. But only if the existing group is willing to listen to the new view and take the risk of being changed. They still need to find a common ground. (And being human is not enough in common!)

Like stacking chairs, we function more smoothly when we gather with like-minded peers.

---

**Bible reading:** Micah 6:6–8.
What does the Lord require?

# Prayer Wheels and Computers

If you travel to Nepal, or Bhutan, or other Buddhist regions of the Himalayas, you're sure to see prayer wheels.

Prayer wheels are colourful cylinders, each containing a written prayer. Every time the cylinder spins, the prayer is supposedly sent out. Everyone passing a prayer wheel is expected to give it a spin. A few enterprising persons dispense with the need for passers-by. Their prayer wheels are kept spinning constantly by the wind, or by tumbling water.

From our scientific Western mindset, the whole idea of prayer wheels seems primitive, even superstitious. But the concept of automated prayer has reached our world too.

A company called Information Age Prayer started a service that will have their computer say a daily prayer for you. For just $3.95 a month. That's only for the Lord's Prayer, of course. If you add morning prayers, prayers for peace or financial help, or up to five get-well prayers, it will cost you more.

As a Protestant, you can get the entire package for just $19.95 a month. That's a bargain. The Jewish package – a *Shema* twice a day, five get-well prayers, and a prayer for peace – goes for $25.95 a month with a *cholim* for the sick or a *Kaddish* for mourning costing extra. The Catholic package, with the complete rosary cycle of Hail Marys and creeds, costs $49.95 a month.

"Show God you are serious!" urges the advertising blurb for the "Full Rosary Package."

"The computer doesn't need any beads to keep track of Hail Marys while saying this prayer," the blurb gushes. "It will be voiced precisely the correct way each time for you without taking any breaks."

To be fair to the company involved, it does not advocate abandoning your own prayers. "Our service should be used... to extend and strengthen a subscriber's connection with God. Traditional prayer...should never be forgone," they caution.

## Musings

But why limit prayers to the speed of human speech? Computers can process digital messages at light speed; is God less capable than a computer?

If I programmed a computer to send prayers constantly, 24 hours a day, transmitted at the speed of light, shouldn't that earn me some serious Air Miles points with God?

Long ago, I read a science fiction story about a Tibetan monastery that decided to jump on the computer bandwagon. The monks had dedicated themselves to reciting all the million possible names of God. When the last name had been named, they believed, the universe would come to an end.

Since computers could process every conceivable combination of letters much faster than humans, the monks enlisted the assistance of some North American programmers. The programmers thought they were just doing a job. But as they walked back down the hill from the monastery, they looked up – and saw the stars winking out, one by one...

Can computers – or prayer wheels, for that matter – really replace human communication? On this issue, I'm with Colin Johnstone. When he was a chaplain with the Canadian Cancer Society, he said, "You can't help a person get well by doing their physical exercises for them, and you can't help someone heal their spirit by trying to do their spiritual exercises for them."

**Bible reading:** Matthew 6:5–14.
The Lord's Prayer.

# Growing Up, Moving On

I don't remember having a kiddie car or a scooter when I was a child. And skateboards hadn't been invented.

But I did have a tricycle. It was blue. A real trike, the British kind, with a chain driving the rear wheels. Once I got it, I could go on the road for a bike ride with my parents. They had to ride slowly, of course, but we could go together.

Inevitably, though, I outgrew my tricycle.

By that time I could ride adult bikes. Sort of. With women's bikes, I simply stood on the pedals – I couldn't reach the seat. Men's bikes demanded more contortions. I rode with one leg stuck through the frame, me leaning one way, the bike the other.

Then one day, I got a two-wheeler of my own. Somewhere, my parents found a bicycle with a small frame. With the seat set as low as it would go, I could just reach the pedals with my toes.

And I left the old blue tricycle behind.

## Musings

We all understand the process that happens during the child and adolescent years. You leave the old teddy bear so that you can lace on skates for hockey. You give up the girl next door for the blonde bombshell, and you give up the bombshell for the girl who becomes your wife. (Granted, that's a male perspective; women's views may not be identical.) You give up roving for fidelity.

It's part of growing up. We call being grown-up, "maturity."

So why do we have so much difficulty applying the same understanding and process to spiritual growth?

All too often, we feel as if we're betraying the truth if we give up ideas taught to us when we were children. I don't mean to belittle children, but children aren't adults. They can't ride adult bicycles yet, and they can't handle adult understandings yet. So we teach them a simplified version. Hopefully, these simplified versions won't prevent them from absorbing a bigger and broader perception of God later in life.

Adults have never told their children everything they know about Santa Claus or the tooth fairy, or sex, work, or money. So why should we assume that what adults told us about God when we were children in Sunday school was the ultimate truth? It was a beginning, a launching pad, a stepping stone.

A friend described some of the crises in her family. "I don't have any faith anymore," she said, sounding almost guilty about it.

I must have looked skeptical. She doesn't act like a woman floundering about trying to find meaning and purpose in her life.

She explained: "I can't – no, I won't – believe in a God who does these things to us."

Good for her. The God she doesn't believe in is the tooth-fairy God she was taught about in her childhood. She's finally leaving her tricycle behind.

---

**Bible reading:** 1 Corinthians 13:9–12.
When I was a child…

# Too Big to Notice

I like travelling by train. They've got more room between seats than planes or buses, and you can get up and move around. They've got bigger windows, too.

What's more, the view's different from those windows. From a plane, you can't see anything except geography or clouds. From a car or bus, you see people's front yards. From a train, you see their backyards.

I've never yet seen a house built to face the railway tracks. People build houses to face roads. This means that when you travel on roads, you see what people want you to see. They put their best yard forward, so to speak. Like a false front on a Wild West store, they try to present a favourable impression.

But backyards are real. They're honest.

Sometimes they're full of broken dreams: the old car rusting quietly away in long grass, the half-built boat, the garden plot taken over by weeds. Sometimes, they're full of hopes for the future: baby clothes hanging on the line, an artist touching up a painting, a girl flying a bright kite. Somehow, as I watch the backyards flicker by, I feel privileged to be peeking into the lives of others.

I remember the first time I had that privileged feeling. I was riding a now defunct little rail line from Kitimat to Terrace, in northeastern British Columbia. As the train slowed through the outskirts of Terrace, a young woman in a bright blue gingham dress reached up to the clothesline over her head and started pinning her family's laundry onto the line.

I watched her. But she never looked up as the train rumbled by.

## Musings

People rarely look as trains go by. Maybe trains are too big, too awesome, to be part of people's lives. It's almost as if the train is an alternate reality that would be disturbing if they actually recognized it.

In that sense, a train is a bit like large governments, corporations, and institutions. Everyone knows they're there. But these organizations do their business at a level somehow divorced from daily life. Ordinary people ignore them and carry on with their private lives as if they exist in a separate world, rather the way ants probably ignore elephants. They have no sense that what they do and talk about in their busy little lives can have any effect or influence on the behemoth that's too big to bother noticing.

Perhaps that's how some people can dutifully attend church on Sunday morning – or the synagogue on Saturday, the mosque on Friday – and dutifully mutter assent to religious doctrines that they ignore the rest of the week. The two worlds don't overlap.

And so they continue cheerfully living in the backyard of their lives, paying no attention to things that rumble by just beyond the edge of their consciousness.

---

**Bible reading:** Exodus 13:20–22.
A pillar of cloud, a pillar of fire.

# THE POWERS WE RELY ON

When the electrical power failed, I was working on a wood-work project. All of a sudden, the high scream of the table saw sagged like a punctured soprano. I flipped the switch. I checked the connections. Nothing brought the saw back to life. It took me a while to realize that all the power, and not just the power going to my saw, was off.

It stayed off for five hours. And I began to realize how much we rely on electrical power these days.

Since I couldn't finish the woodworking project in the garage, I went upstairs to see if I could get some news about what had happened. But the TV wouldn't turn on. No power.

The portable radio had batteries. But since this was a weekend, most of the local broadcasting outlets were reading wire service news out of Ontario. On the local CBC station, only national programs were running.

I've never understood why media newsrooms expect news to happen only during their Monday to Friday daytime shifts. Disasters do not, in my experience, lend themselves to prior scheduling. But that's a digression.

I tried to check my e-mail. Of course, the computer was dead. I tried to make myself a cup of tea. The kettle wouldn't work. Neither would the stove, or the microwave. This seemed like a good time to practice my rudimentary *Piano Lessons for Older Beginners*. But it's an electric keyboard. No sound.

In fact, hardly anything worked without electricity – the vacuum cleaner, the washer, the dryer, the refrigerator, the dishwasher, the air-conditioning, Joan's sewing machine and serger, my woodcarving tools, even all but one of our telephones. Without electricity, we were as helpless as newborn babes without their parents.

I went for a walk. The street was uncommonly silent. No power tools screaming. No boomboxes blaring. No music at all, in fact, except for one person sitting on her porch attempting a few simple tunes on a harmonica.

Lacking electricity, life reverted to simpler patterns. People gathered in lawn chairs on their patios, enjoying the fading light of evening. Others stood around in the street chatting, instead of rushing to appointments.

## Musings

Back in the days when I taught Sunday school, I sometimes used the analogy that God was like electricity. Both were invisible forces that we could only recognize by the effect they had. Electricity moved motors and meters; it made filaments heat up; it transmitted energy. But we couldn't actually see electricity – only what it did.

Similarly, we could recognize God only by the way God affected people, who then applied their energy to create justice, or love, or beauty.

The power failure made me wonder if electricity has become more than just an illustration of God. Maybe it has become the new almighty power that we worship.

Which one has more influence over our daily lives? Which one could we more easily do without?

---

**Bible reading:** Matthew 25:31–45.
Separating the sheep and the goats.

# Dragons and Demons

Once upon a time, in the general manner of these old tales, there was a handsome young prince. He heard of a beautiful princess imprisoned in a tower, waiting to be rescued by a handsome prince like him. But between him and her lay a deep, dark forest populated with evil demons and fierce fire-breathing dragons who didn't like handsome princes.

But the handsome prince was confident. So he fought his way through the forest. Sometimes, he had to resort to trickery and deceit. He slaughtered, he slew, he swindled, he murdered. But after years of constant battle with the forces of evil, he emerged on the far side of the forest into gorgeous gardens.

And there stood the tower, from which he would free the beautiful princess.

He looked at himself, still dripping with the blood of the last dragon, and decided to clean up a little before ringing the princess's doorbell. So he stopped at a pool to wash and shave.

In the water, he saw his own reflection.

The years of battling evil with its own weapons had taken its toll. The face that looked back at him was lined with anger, with hate, with venom. He had won, but at what price? He was now no different than those he had slain in what he thought was a noble cause.

He was no longer a handsome young prince.

So he slunk back into the deep, dark forest.

## Musings

I don't know where that story came from, but I find myself returning over and over to the profound truth within it.

I believe that there is purpose and meaning in this universe, that we are not just accidental assemblies of energy fields. And purpose and meaning must have a goal, an intention. Out of my cultural background, I think of that goal as the Kingdom of God – a setting of peace, goodwill, and harmony.

Many factors – and many people – get in the way of peace, goodwill, and harmony. And I'm tempted to battle them, to destroy them, using any means available to me.

But resorting to the enemy's tactics to defeat the enemy won't work. The end never justifies the means.

This quotation showed up on a newspaper page I almost used for lighting the fireplace one evening. Just before I crumpled the paper up, I saw these lines. They come from Jim Grant, former Executive Director of UNICEF.

> This is the true joy in life, being used for a purpose... I am of the opinion that my life belongs to the whole community, and, as long as I live, it is my privilege to do for it whatever I can. I rejoice in life for its own sake. Life is no brief candle to me. It is a sort of splendid torch which I have gotten hold of for the moment, and I want to make it burn as brightly as possible before handing it on to future generations.

---

**Bible reading:** Romans 12:1–7.
Be transformed, not conformed.

# A TWIST IN THE TALE

Sometimes familiar stories get too familiar. We start thinking that's how it has to be. So let's try retelling one of those stories.

It was Christmas Eve, see. And these guys, they had to work the night shift at the warehouse, shipping out thousands of leftover Christmas parcels.

All of a sudden, a guy at the loading dock called out, "Hey, come take a look at this!"

When they looked out at the night sky, it was like every molecule of air was dancing, leaving a fluorescent trail in its path. And the guys all said, "Wow!"

Other people in town saw the same thing. But they said, "Interesting phenomenon. I must check the Internet to see if there's a reasonable scientific explanation." And they went back inside.

But the warehouse guys kept watching.

Soon they started hearing white noise, like whispering that was too far away to make out the words. But after a while they were sure they could hear some words. And the words said something like, "Don't be afraid. A child is being born, right now, a child who can save the world."

"Why should I believe you?" one of the warehouse guys asked.

"No one has to believe me," the words in the sky seemed to say. "But if you go to the motel in town, you'll find that baby and his mother huddled under the stairs to one of the units. And when you see them, maybe you'll believe."

And then the cascade of voices seemed to swell into a great chorus, singing, "Glory to God, and peace on earth, for God cares about humans."

Everyone could have heard the chorus. But most people were too busy to pay attention. Some were making too much noise at their Christmas parties. Others had the TV turned up loud. And a lot just closed their windows to shut out sounds they didn't want to hear.

But the guys locked up the warehouse. "The parcels can wait," they said. They commandeered a company van, and roared off to the motel. Where they found a newborn baby. Wrapped up in his daddy's windbreaker. With his mother. Huddled under a balcony, to keep out of the rain.

And then the warehouse guys believed.

So they gave the family some blankets from the truck. And their own winter jackets. And a Thermos of hot coffee.

But they couldn't keep the good news to themselves. So they drove back through town at 2:00 a.m. with their truck windows down, honking the horn and banging on the doors of the truck, yelling, "It's a boy!"

And a lot more people slammed their windows shut. A few even called the cops about the disturbance.

## Musings

The good news was available to everyone. But only the warehouse guys did four things that allowed them to hear it.

- They paid attention.
- They kept their minds open.
- They risked acting on their intuitions.
- And they couldn't keep their discovery to themselves.

It's so simple. So why do so many of us still shut our windows and devote our attention to other things?

---

**Bible reading:** Luke 2:6–20.
The Nativity story.

# APPENDIX

From the Introduction to the first volume of *Everyday Parables* (Wood Lake Books, 1995).

In a sense, this book is a beginner's guide to theological reflection. Having me do your theological reflection for you is as useless as having me do your aerobic exercises for you. It may do me a lot of good, but it won't do you any good at all.

So what's in this book is 128 pages of starter kit. It's a set of booster cables. It's *Coles' Notes* on theological reflection on everyday life.

The point is simply this: I believe that the vast majority of Christians today have given up expecting to discern God most of the time. The more technologically complex the world into which people are born, the less likely they are to get involved in religion.

A few years ago, some friends and I sat at a table at Tim Faller's wedding reception. His great-grandmother sat across the table from us. She was 99 years old. She'd been born a decade before the turn of the century. In her lifetime, she has seen the advent of air flight, of cars, of telephones, of recorded music, of radio and television, of transistors and computers, of electricity, of petroleum fuels...The world she was born into knew nothing of ozone depletion or acid rain or global warming. It had never been threatened by nuclear warfare. Forests and the fish were considered inexhaustible.

There has been more change in this century than in all the other 19 centuries since the time of Jesus. At the turn of the last century, people still lived pretty much as biblical people did. They might work in heavy industry, but in their homes they still used lamps and hand tools that people from biblical times could recognize.

But what would biblical people make of a modern dishwasher? Or a microwave oven? Or a stereo set playing compact discs that reproduce the sound of a full orchestra and chorus?

I can still remember enough of that former world that the stories of the Bible mean something to me. But how much can a teenager born into the computer age, a young adult born since the Vietnam War, a child who has never known a time when people did not have satellites hovering in the sky – how much can these newcomers have in common with a community of people who express their faith mostly in images of a long-ago time?

The problem is not that the story of God, the message of Jesus, is out of date. The problem is that we Christians have been content to express that story in outdated images and metaphors. We've been content to let someone else – a few years or a few centuries ago – do our theological reflection for us.

As a community of faith, the stories we tell imply that God is not present in this world. God was there in biblical times. God may have been there during the medieval period, and during the Reformation. God may be revealed in the German theological colleges of the early part of this century, or in the barrios and *favelas* of Latin America or in the unspoiled wilderness of a national park. But God is not here in our four-wheel drive SUVs, our iPods, or GPS navigation systems.

Because we simply do not talk about God when we talk about those things. Whatever our doctrines affirm, our stories reveal that God is irrelevant to 90% of our lives.

So this book is a "beginner's guide," because if we are to start telling stories that include God in our daily world, we have to start with the seemingly insignificant stuff. The everyday stuff that's so common we habitually overlook it. There is no point in practicing theological reflection about international politics when we can't do theological reflection about peeling potatoes.

Things really matter only when they hit close to home. I've watched church assemblies pass resolutions without a dissenting voice that instruct national governments to change their monetary policies or to get rid of racial discrimination. The heated debate comes over the choice of music for worship, whether congregations can be required to accept a gay minister, and who gets the TV remote.

Jesus did not build his parables on what one head of state said to another head of state. He talked about ordinary, everyday things. In them, he found evidence of the nature and purpose of God.

So must we.

The profound theologizing must come not when I write these words, but when you read them. It will come not from my thoughts but from yours. You may well look at these parables and say, "A potato peeler? A door hinge? A pair of shoelaces? What's religious about those things?" But you may remember that there's nothing particularly religious about sheep, or vines, or salt either. We only give significance to these everyday things when we associate them with religious truths.

In the same way, we will give significance to every aspect of our lives when we associate those things with what we know of God and the church, of Jesus and our faith.

Jim Taylor

# LIST OF READINGS

| BIBLE READING | BIBLICAL SUBJECT | TITLE OF BOOK PARABLE | PAGE # |
|---|---|---|---|
| Genesis 3:16–24 | Banished from the Garden of Eden | Goodbye to Eden | 19 |
| Genesis 6:5–7, 9:8–11 | God's covenant with Noah | Pears and People | 17 |
| Exodus 13:20–22 | Pillar of cloud, pillar of fire | Too Big to Notice | 130 |
| Exodus 34:27–30, | Moses' face shines | Encountering the Holy | 113 |
| Deuteronomy 30:15–20a | Choose life | Acts of Protest | 83 |
| Psalm 103:15–18 | Mortality | Foolhardy Actions | 41 |
| Psalm 139:1–6 | Known intimately | The Ultimate Audience | 102 |
| Proverbs 6:6–8 | Look to the ant | Monkeying Around | 69 |
| Isaiah 11:1–5 | New shoots from strong roots | Strong Roots, New Shoots | 55 |
| Isaiah 40:28–31 | Rise on wings like eagles | Soaring Fearlessly | 45 |
| Isaiah 43:18–19 | God does a new thing | Doing Things Differently | 105 |
| Micah 6:6–8 | What does the Lord require? | Stacking Chairs | 122 |
| Matthew 5:21–22, 27–28, 31–34a, 38–41 | You have heard it said, but I say… | Restoring the Original | 119 |
| Matthew 5:21–24 | Make peace with your brother or sister | Buried Scars | 35 |
| Matthew 6:5–14 | The Lord's Prayer | Prayer Wheels and Computers | 125 |
| Matthew 7:13–14 | Enter by the narrow gate | Living with Ambiguity | 110 |
| Matthew 12:46–50 | Who is my family? | In Our Element | 75 |

| BIBLE READING | BIBLICAL SUBJECT | TITLE OF BOOK PARABLE | PAGE # |
|---|---|---|---|
| Matthew 13:24–30 | The weeds among the wheat | Leaving a Legacy | 23 |
| Matthew 13:3–9 | Parable of the Sower | Introduction | 10 |
| Matthew 18:15–20 | Gathering people for a purpose | Meetings and More Meetings | 95 |
| Matthew 25:31–45 | Separating sheep and goats | The Powers We Rely On | 133 |
| Mark 3:1–5 | The man with a withered hand | Contradictory Impulses | 57 |
| Mark 4:1–9 | Parable of the Sower | Introduction | 10 |
| Mark 4:1–9 | Parable of the Sower | Seeds and Sowers | 29 |
| Mark 7:28 | Dogs under the table | Chapter intro | 43 |
| Mark 10:13–16 | Like a little child | Our Heavenly Grandparent | 100 |
| Luke 2:6–20 | The Nativity story | A Twist in the Tale | 137 |
| Luke 8:4–8 | Parable of the Sower | Introduction | 10 |
| Luke 9:51–56 | Refusal to call down fire | The Gentle Giant | 47 |
| Luke 12:6 | Value of sparrows | Chapter intro | 43 |
| Luke 12:6–7 | God values even sparrows | On Eagle's Wings | 65 |
| Luke 13:18–24 | Series of parables | Introduction | 7 |
| Luke 13:1–9 | A second chance | Adversarial Systems | 85 |
| Luke 15:11–32 | Prodigal Son | Introduction | 10 |
| Luke 16:10–13 | Honesty in small things | Watch for the Magpies | 52 |
| Luke 22:14–20 | The Last Supper | God's Doorknobs | 63 |
| John 19:25–27 | Behold your son | The Useless Emotion | 67 |

| Bible Reading | Biblical Subject | Title of Book Parable | Page # |
|---|---|---|---|
| John 21:15–17 | Passing on the Shepherd's role | Rescuing Lost Logs | 91 |
| Acts 2:1–4 | The coming of the Holy Spirit | Northern Lights | 33 |
| Acts 17:24–28 | The one in whom we live and move | The Law of Gravity | 39 |
| Romans 12:1–7 | Be transformed, not conformed | Dragons and Demons | 135 |
| 1 Corinthians 13:1–4 | If I do not have love | Big Rocks First | 107 |
| 1 Corinthians 13:1–7 | If I do not have love | The Words Don't Matter | 117 |
| 1 Corinthians 13:9–12 | When I was a child... | Growing Up, Moving On | 127 |
| 1 Corinthians 15:12–20 | Raised from the dead | Homely Resurrections | 98 |
| Philippians 2:5–10 | Having the mind of Christ | Acting in Unison | 60 |
| Philippians 4:4–7 | Rejoice in the Lord | Attitude of Gratitude | 49 |
| 1 Thessalonians 5:12–22 | Pray without ceasing | Praying without Words | 79 |
| Hebrews 6:17–20a | An unchangeable promise | Fixed Focus | 27 |
| 1 John 4:16b–21 | Perfect love casts out fear | Irrational Reactions | 73 |
| Revelation 3:1b–2, 15–17 | Neither hot nor cold | Shades of Human Nature | 88 |
| Revelation 18:8–10 | Babylon fallen into fire | Blessings and Curses | 25 |